HEALTH BY DESIGN

A BIBLICAL APPROACH

DR. BILLY MELOT

WESTBOW
PRESS®
A DIVISION OF THOMAS NELSON
& ZONDERVAN

The information, ideas, and suggestions in this book are not intended as a substitute for professional medical advice. Before following any suggestions contained in this book, you should consult your personal physician. Neither the author nor the publisher shall be liable or responsible for any loss or damage allegedly arising as a consequence of your use or application of any information or suggestions in this book.

WestBow Press books may be ordered through booksellers or by contacting:

WestBow Press
A Division of Thomas Nelson & Zondervan
1663 Liberty Drive
Bloomington, IN 47403
www.westbowpress.com
1 (866) 928-1240

Because of the dynamic nature of the Internet, any web addresses or links contained in this book may have changed since publication and may no longer be valid. The views expressed in this work are solely those of the author and do not necessarily reflect the views of the publisher, and the publisher hereby disclaims any responsibility for them.

Any people depicted in stock imagery provided by Getty Images are models, and such images are being used for illustrative purposes only. Certain stock imagery © Getty Images.

ISBN: 978-1-9736-7906-6 (sc)
ISBN: 978-1-9736-7907-3 (hc)
ISBN: 978-1-9736-7905-9 (e)

Library of Congress Control Number: 2019917596

Print information available on the last page.

WestBow Press rev. date: 10/30/2019

If the Bible is true and truth sets us free, then the Bible has the power to transform all areas of our lives: the way we walk, talk, eat, drink, work, live, and love. Everything can have profound and eternal effects on our lives. Jesus said when we gather together to eat and drink, "Do this in remembrance of me." Let's celebrate our food and drink in a way that honors our lives and health!

CONTENTS

ACKNOWLEDGMENTS

Thank you to my wonderful, supportive wife, Brooke Melot. Thanks for being so loving and encouraging. Thanks for working so hard for our family and always putting others first. Thanks for being such a strong, godly woman. I look forward to spending the rest of my life with you, and I can't wait to see what all God has planned for our future.

Thank you to my father for being such an involved father. You taught me so much about life, masculinity, work ethic, conviction, and so much more. Thanks for working so hard to provide for our large family and for teaching me so many life skills, which are too many to list here! I will never forget all of the memories we had together when I was young and am excited for all of the life experiences that God will provide in the future. I will always try to pass that knowledge to my children so your legacy will continue as prescribed in Psalm 78:4, "We will not hide them from their children but tell to the coming generation the glorious deeds of the Lord, and His might, and the wonders that he has done."

Thank you to my mother for raising me in such a loving, godly environment and for nurturing, loving, supporting, and feeding me as well as putting up with me. You taught me so much about life. You always bring laughter to every situation. You are a seemingly endless source of joy and comfort for us children and a glue that holds the family together. You are the best mother a son could ask for! You sacrificed so much for the family, and I will never forget all that you have done for me.

Thank you to all of my siblings for all of your love and support all of these years: Sarah, Melissa, Katherine, Rebecca, Kristi, Elizabeth, John David, and Emily. I love you all. Thank you to my brothers-in-law for the help, support, and technical assistance in my various projects. I look forward to many more years of shenanigans.

Thank you to the doctors who have mentored me throughout my career. You all taught me so much about life, work, attitude, clinical etiquette, and so on. I could not be where I am today without standing on the shoulders of giants. Thank you.

Thank you to my life coach and counselor, Cathy Teague. I can never repay you for the amount of help you have provided me with my personal growth, emotional healing, and relational development. Thank you to my friend and spiritual mentor, Rabbi Yisreal Avraham. You have taught me so much about God, life, prayer, and holy mind-set.

Thank you to Dr. Dean Mathis for many years of spiritually mentoring. Thank you for leading my ordination into ministry, for providing my first opportunity to serve the church, and for officiating my wedding. I tremendously appreciate how you ministered to my parents when they were going through their tribulations.

Thank you to Andrew Wheat for being a spiritual solid rock in my life all of these years and business partner for Paradigm Bible Games. It's been quite an adventure!

INTRODUCTION

Today nutrition and health care are multibillion-dollar industries, with everything imaginable being marketed as healthy, safe, or effective. Yet despite these claims and the size of the industry, we have become one of the unhealthiest countries on earth. Somewhere, something has gone terribly wrong with our system. Our trauma care is the most progressive, and our technology allows us to prolong the quantity of our days, but what about our quality of life? Many would argue that our quality of life is decreasing. Despite the best efforts of our health-care system, research has shown that we are one of the unhealthiest countries on earth.

Chronic physical diseases have become so common that they are considered normal in American society, and diseases are developing at younger ages than previous generations. For example, four out of five Americans will suffer from back pain, the most common cause of disability and the second-most common health-related reason that people miss work. One-third of Americans will suffer from chronic neck pain. The United States also has some of the highest incidences of obesity, cancer, heart disease, diabetes, and stroke per capita in the world. We have the most people in hospitals per capita and spend the most money per capita on health than any other country in the world, spending three times more money on health care than the next highest-spending country.

In America, there are 70 million people with arthritis, 39 million with chronic allergies, 17 million with asthma, 60 million with cardiovascular disease, and millions more who suffer from cancers, diabetes, autoimmune diseases, neurological disorders, and other chronic degenerative diseases.

In addition, America consumes far more pharmaceutical drugs per capita than any other country, with half of all American adults taking a prescription medication every week. Americans consume 75 percent of the world's supply of pharmaceutical drugs,[1] 80 percent of the world's prescription opioids (painkillers), and 99 percent of all hydrocodone.[2] This is astounding considering we comprise less than 5 percent of the world's total population. In fact, more people will die in the United States from prescription painkiller overdoses than all illegal narcotics combined. The average American over the age of sixty is taking at least eight prescription drugs, often with half of those being prescribed to manage the side effects from the others. Tragically, 100,000 Americans die every year from properly prescribed, properly taken prescription drugs.[3]

Physical diseases are only part of the health problem. Neurological, neurodegenerative, and neurobehavioral diseases have also been escalating. Autism has increased by 78 percent in the past ten years.[4] Alzheimer's disease has been increasing and is expected to continue increasing by 44 percent across the United States within the next decade.[5] Psychological disorders are also on the rise by disastrous numbers, along with the damages associated with them, such as suicides and homicides, the second- and third-leading cause of death in teenagers.

The fastest-growing pharmaceutical drug category is antipsychotics targeting mental health disorders in teenagers and young adults, with a growth rate of 13 percent per year.[6] 6.7 percent of Americans are clinically depressed[7] with many modern technologies accelerating these risks. For example, social media platforms have been linked to higher rates of depression, anxiety, and emotional disconnection. Two thirds of all Americans now use at least one social media platform, and 94 percent of young adults participate in social media.

Despite these tools, American social health is on the decline. People are communicating, socializing, and critically thinking less. According to the National Endowment for the Arts, reading comprehension has declined by 10 percent over the past twenty years and continues to decrease.

Americans have some of the highest death rates due to lifestyle-oriented diseases in the world. Every year, 611,105 Americans die from cardiovascular disease, 584,881 from cancer, 149,205 from chronic lower respiratory disease, 128,978 from stroke, and 75,578 from diabetes. Many of these cases could have been prevented or reversed through lifestyle changes.

Many people have been taught to believe that genetics are the cause of these diseases, yet these trends have only developed in the last few decades. This begs the question: are there other factors that influence our health?

And do we have control over them? Can environmental factors—such as lifestyle, diet, and exercise—change the state of our health? The answer is absolutely yes!

God revealed His knowledge and wisdom to mankind through the Bible so we could understand more about ourselves and the world around us. Therefore, the answers to our current health crisis can be found within God's holy written Word. The Bible, backed by sound science, can provide a robust plan for our health and reveal to us the way that God designed our health from the beginning of creation.

CORRUPTED SCIENCE

The problem with modern health science is not God, but mankind's limited—and sometimes corrupt—knowledge. Proverbs 14:12 says, "There is a way which seems right to a man, but in the end it leads to destruction."

From the beginning of history, there have been numerous occasions where an action seemed right to mankind and afterwards was found to be destructive. In Genesis 3:5 (NIV), the serpent (Satan) said to Eve, "For God knows that when you eat from it [the tree of the knowledge of good and evil] your eyes will be opened, and you will be like God." In her limited understanding, she disobeyed God, ate the fruit, and then shared it with Adam.

Fast-forward to Genesis 11:4 (NIV) in which the people of Babel decided to "build ... a tower that reaches to the heavens, so that [they] may make a name for [themselves]." So they ignored God's command to "have no other gods before me" (Exodus 20:3 NIV), and as a result, they became scattered and divided. This has continued, generation after generation, throughout history.

In the Middle Ages, the scientific community believed that the world was flat, a misconception that was addressed several times in the Bible. Isaiah 40:22 (NIV) reads, "He sits enthroned above the circle of the earth." The Bible stated that the world was round over a thousand years before Pythagoras, Columbus, or Magellan. So for over a millennium, misguided thought hindered mankind's exploration of the earth, as sailors were too afraid to travel far from land for fear of falling off the planet.

In the eighteenth and nineteenth centuries, bloodletting was considered a standard medical procedure. Bloodletting, or blood leeching, was the process of attaching a living leech to the skin of a human to parasitically suck the blood from a diseased part of the body. The Bible directly taught against such practices in Leviticus 17:11 (NIV) when it stated, "The life of a creature is in the blood." As a result of this erroneous medical practice, millions of people throughout history were seriously and critically injured, including George Washington, the first president of the United States. Science has since proven that this procedure is completely ineffective, demonstrating again that the Bible is profoundly scientific.

People can be deceived because of limitations in perspective.

1. People cannot see past the physical area that they currently occupy. They have no idea what is happening outside their house, across town, in other cities, or around the globe.
2. People cannot see into the future.
3. People have no experience of the past before their existence. People require third-party information from others to construct a worldview, which leaves them susceptible to deceit or mistakes.

Within the context of our modern health-care system, it is easy to see how false information can misguide people. There are large financial incentives for companies to withhold harmful information from their research.

- In 2012, pharmaceutical megacorporation GlaxoSmithKline was fined $3 billion after pleading guilty to bribing doctors, encouraging prescriptions of unsuitable antidepressants to children, and failing to inform the public that these drugs caused teenagers to become suicidal.
- In 2015, Martin Shkreli, CEO of Turing Pharmaceuticals, was arrested for securities fraud after increasing the price of his drug from $13.50 to $750 per dose, a 5,456 percent increase, in order to profit from the insurance system.
- In 1986, the US government formed the National Vaccine Injury Compensation (NVIC) Program to reduce the burden of lawsuits upon the pharmaceutical industry due to the sheer volume of vaccine injuries and deaths that had been and continue to occur. Roughly six hundred cases per year have been filed with the NVIC, totaling over $3.4 billion in payouts to families damaged by the side effects of vaccines.[8]
- A study published in the *Journal of American Medical Association Internal Medicine* found widespread falsification (lying) and blatant corruption within clinical trials performed by the Food

and Drug Administration (FDA) when they were approving new drugs for public use. In the study, researchers concluded,

Fifty-seven published clinical trials were identified for which an FDA inspection of a trial site had found significant evidence of 1 or more of the following problems: falsification or submission of false information, 22 trials (39%); problems with adverse events reporting, 14 trials (25%); protocol violations, 42 trials (74%); inadequate or inaccurate recordkeeping, 35 trials (61%); failure to protect the safety of patients and/or issues with oversight or informed consent, 30 trials (53%); and violations not otherwise categorized, 20 trials (35%). Only 3 of the 78 publications (4%) that resulted from trials in which the FDA found significant violations mentioned the objectionable conditions or practices found during the inspection. No corrections, retractions, expressions of concern, or other comments acknowledging the key issues identified by the inspection were subsequently published.[9]

To paraphrase: the government admits that there is corruption in the regulation of drugs developed in our current medical system. God warned of corruption in Hosea 4:6 (NIV). "My people are destroyed for lack of knowledge; because you have rejected knowledge, I reject you from being a priest to me. And since you have forgotten the law of your God, I also will forget your children."

King Solomon recognized the importance of correct knowledge and stated, "Wisdom is better than rubies, and nothing compares to it!" (Proverbs 8:11 KJV). It is important to seek out truthful information, to be well informed and educated so the "truth will set you free" (John 8:32 NIV).

The Bible is necessary to discern the truth from misinformation. It was written by over 40 authors, spanning 1,500 years throughout almost 100 generations, and has never changed. It has one common theme: the revelation and salvation of God to His creation. The Bible has proven itself to be consistently true and compatible with science. It is the juxtaposition to all of the problems that arise from corrupted science. The Bible can help create a robust and comprehensive plan for our health that is far superior to any other diet plan because it illustrates the lifestyle that God designed for creation from the beginning of time.

GOD'S PLAN

In the Bible, King David writes, "For you created my inmost being; you knit me together in my mother's womb … Your eyes saw my unformed body; all the days ordained for me were written in your book before one of them came to be" (Psalm 139:13,16 NIV). He acknowledged that God created each person and knows every subtle detail about them. God knows more about our health than anything because He created us. One would not take a broken cell phone to a lawn mower factory to repair it or purchase a new appliance and discard the instructions before assembling it, yet people disregard the Bible and its health instructions all the time. The Bible contains over a hundred verses about health, and they are all congruent with science. God's simple instruction is to obey His laws and benefit from their blessings.

People have often told me, "Dr. Melot, those dietary laws seem outdated and unnecessary. Why would God put such restrictions on my life?"

It's a great question. God's instructions in the Bible were intended to benefit us, not restrict us. 1 John 5:3 (NIV) says, "This is love for God: to keep his commands. And <u>His commands are not burdensome</u>." Every single health law written in the Bible is congruent with nutritional and medical science. There is a measurable benefit to people who follow the instructions and detriment to those who don't.

The Bible warns against turning away from God's design and following another plan. "Cursed is the one who trusts in man, who draws strength from mere flesh and whose heart turns away from the LORD" (Jeremiah 17:5 NIV). Since God knows every inner working part of our body, any other plan would be less than ideal. Proverbs 3:5 (NIV) tells us, "Trust in the LORD with all your heart and lean not on your own understanding; in all your ways acknowledge Him, and He will make your paths straight."

If you want a truly healthy life, then the best approach is God's approach. He never promised an easy, pain-free, or trial-free life (James 1:2–4), but He does promise that we can be free of chronic diseases. Twenty-three times in the Old Testament, God promises good health to those who obey His commands (His dietary and sanitation laws).

In Daniel, God challenged the mightiest civilization of the time. Daniel told his captors, "Test your servants for ten days. Give us nothing but vegetables to eat and water to drink. Then compare our appearance with that of the young men who eat the royal food and treat your servants in accordance with what you see" (1:12). At the end of Daniel's test, he and his friends "looked healthier and better nourished than any of the young men who ate the royal food" (Daniel 1:15), and God blessed Daniel with "knowledge and understanding of all kinds of literature and learning" (Daniel 1:17).

I encourage you to consider this challenge for your own life: to test His nutritional blessings so you can personally experience the divine wisdom, healing power, and incredible design of God for your life.

DIVINE DESIGN

To begin to fully understand our health, we must start at the beginning with the design of mankind. Our society, for the most part, has adopted the Greco-Roman philosophy of "self," known as dualism. This concept has matriculated down from the Greek and Roman empires, which existed hundreds of years ago. In this philosophy, humans exist as two equal but opposing compartments, the body and the soul. The body would consist of its physical properties: size, shape, weight, color, and so on. The soul would consist of everything ethereal or nonphysical, such as thoughts, emotions, or feelings.

The Bible describes human existence as something else entirely. The Bible tells us that people were created as a perfect reflection of God's image. Since God exists in a trinity of three parts, people were created with three aspects to our nature: the body, the soul, and the spirit (1 Thessalonians 5:23). These dimensions are neither mutually exclusive nor opposing to each other as the Greco-Roman culture believed; rather they are all intimately connected to each other. Consequently each part of our nature directly affects the other parts and vice versa. So you cannot achieve physical health without spiritual health, emotional health without physical health, and so on and so forth. Consider the following Bible verses in this context:

- I pray that you may enjoy good health and that all may go well with you, even as your soul is getting along well. (3 John 1:2 NIV)
- A cheerful heart is good medicine, but a crushed spirit dries up the bones. (Proverbs 17:22 NIV)
- Gracious words are a honeycomb, sweet to the soul and healing to the bones. (Proverbs 16:24 NIV)

- Do you not know that your bodies are temples of the Holy Spirit, who is in you, whom you have received from God? (1 Corinthians 6:19–20 NIV)
- If you listen carefully to the LORD your God and do what is right in his eyes, if you pay attention to his commands and keep his decrees, I will not bring on you any of the diseases I brought upon the Egyptians, for I am the LORD, who heals you. (Exodus 15:26 NIV)
- Present your bodies as a living sacrifice, holy and acceptable to God, which is your spiritual worship. (Romans 12:1 ESV)
- Be transformed by the renewing of your mind. (Romans 12:2 NIV)

Hundreds of other Bible verses further illustrate this idea. The Bible makes it very clear that humans exist as three-dimensional creatures. Science also supports this concept. Here are four very succinct examples from nature:

1. A phenomenon known as the widowhood effect, or broken heart syndrome, has been widely observed and documented throughout history. It occurs when a person's death occurs at almost exactly the same time as their intimate partner, for no explainable medical reason. One partner has no medical trauma, no major health problem, and no physically recognizable reason to pass away at that time. They simply died of heartbreak due to their companion passing away. There are many well-documented cases of this phenomenon and even many high-profile examples such as June Carter Cash and Johnny Cash and George and Barbara Bush. This phenomenon is so well recognized that it is often used as a plot device (an event that drives a story) for books and movies: *The Notebook* (Noah and Allie), *Where the Red Fern Grows* (Old Dan and Little Ann), and *Star Wars Episode III* (Padme and Anakin). Many people, when asked, have observed this phenomenon in family members or friends. Interestingly, broken heart syndrome reinforces the idea that people have a spiritual aspect to their nature, their existences become one when they become married (Genesis 2; Ephesians 5), and their spiritual nature is deeply connected to their physical nature.

2. The next scientific example has to do with epidemiological studies about cancer survival. Epidemiology is the branch of medicine that

studies how and why certain diseases happen to the population. Multiple population studies have demonstrated that people who believed in God had substantially better cancer survival rates. The Moffitt Cancer Center and colleagues collected all available research written on the topic and combined them into a meta-analysis that included over 32,000 cancer patients of various cancer types, stages of development, and treatment protocols. They comprehensively concluded that over 70 percent of cancer patients actively engage in prayer and there was a direct link between a higher spiritual well-being and better physical health. Afterwards, cancer.org added "having a spiritual connection," the blandest way to acknowledge the power of God's healing power in the universe, as an official part of a comprehensive cancer treatment plan.

3. Next is the well-documented association between physical activity and mental health. An overwhelming majority of medical studies on this topic, dating all the way back to the 1980s, when they first started doing research on the subject, conclude that exercise is a strong mood enhancer and mental health stabilizer. It reduces stress, improves mood, increases self-esteem, enhances creativity, sharpens memory, and so on and so forth. Exercise dramatically improves—and in some cases even totally alleviates—cases of mild to moderate clinical depression. Twenty-five other medical studies reveal that exercise can help prevent or reduce depression from occurring in the first place. With regard to anxiety disorders, scientific research papers about anxiety, specifically nearly fifty published medical studies, conclude that physical activity is as or more effective than prescription medication for reducing symptoms and severity of anxiety. Regular exercise has also been shown to counteract cognitive decline as people age.[10] There is a very strong correlation between mental and spiritual health and physical exercise.

4. The last example deals with how our mental state affects our physical abilities. In 1996, Dr. Blaslotto of the University of Chicago performed a study on mental visualization. He separated test subjects into three groups and tested each group's ability to shoot a basketball into the hoop from the free throw line. After the initial test, he asked the first group to not touch a basketball for thirty days. The second group was asked to practice shooting

free throws for thirty minutes daily. The last group was asked to go to the gym, close their eyes, and mentally visualize shooting the basketball for thirty minutes daily, but not practice. After thirty days, he retested every group. Group one showed no improvement in their basketball skills. Group two improved their ability to make free throws by 24 percent. Astoundingly, group three improved their basketball shooting percentage by 23 percent. They improved nearly as much as the group who practiced every day without ever touching the ball. As a result, almost every professional athletic organization now implements some sort of mental visualization into their practice routine. They have taken pure science, without any biblical bias, and made it applicable to create physical competitive advantage. Science supports the biblical concept that human nature consists of multiple dimensions and that these dimensions are unequivocally linked.

God's design for human existence is fundamentally different than the Greco-Roman perspective because it involves the whole person: the physical, mental, and spiritual. God's design for human life is much more profound, and His design for health involves more than a meditation plan, prescription pill, or fitness trend. It includes the whole person, not just a part. True God-designed health is the all-encompassing, uninhibited pursuit of purpose for your life.

ETERNAL ENGINEERING

Because we are designed as a perfect reflection of God, the divine, our bodies were created perfectly. And they do contain the most complex biological processes on the planet. The human brain has more connections and a larger memory capacity than the entire World Wide Web.[11] Each cell in the body is more complex than the largest factory on earth. The intrinsic opioids (pain relievers) are ten times more powerful than morphine, yet not addictive.[12] A developing baby will double in size in the first six months.[13] In addition, the collective human ability to discover and learn new things is amazing: it is estimated that all discoverable knowledge doubles every few years.[14] Consider the past 150 years. We have invented ways to drive, fly, communicate worldwide, and explore space.

The most meaningful attribute about us is that we were created to live forever. God designed our bodies to be self-healing. Think back to the last time you suffered a cut or scrape. It initially bled and then scabbed, and eventually the scab fell away, leaving only a scar, which itself would also fade over time. You did not have to consciously tell your body to repair itself. It did so on its own. Instead it was programmed from the beginning to heal itself.

Contrast that with an automobile that was in a fender bender. It remained broken until an outside influence repaired it. In fact, even without a fender bender, it will break down with time and use.

Everything else on earth breaks down when used, except for the human body. If you stress a muscle, it grows back stronger. If you stress or even break a bone, it heals stronger. If you present the brain with a new stimulus, it will develop new neuronal connections. (It will learn and adapt.) If you work the heart, it gets healthier. In fact, human beings are the only things on the planet that actually improve with use.

Research suggests that the sedimentary lifestyle is a major contributing factor for every major chronic disease, and a lack of physical and mental stimulus actually decreases our health. God designed us this way because we were created "in His image" with the capability to live and fulfill His purposes forever.

Scientifically speaking, how do our bodies continue to repair themselves naturally? On a cellular level, our bodies are constantly and continually replacing old, damaged, and unwanted cells with new, vibrant, and healthy ones. This is nonstop from the day we were conceived until the day we die. It happens one cell at a time, but at an incredibly fast pace, allowing the body to sluff off and replace entire portions of the body that are sick, unhealthy, or diseased. So when you go to your favorite restaurant and sit across from your significant other for the hundredth time in your life and you look across and sweetly gaze into their eyes, reminiscing on the old times, you are, ironically enough, looking at a completely different body than you did the first time you laid eyes on them, yet it is still the same person.

This is great news for those who need healing. God has programmed our bodies to replace damaged portions of themselves—cells, tissues, and even whole organs, one cell at a time, in order to constantly heal themselves. For example, our bodies produce millions of new blood cells every second. The two largest organs—the skin and the liver—replace themselves entirely every few months. The heart, which was once thought to be unable to regenerate, is now shown to proliferate (produce new healthy cells) after severe damage, such as heart attack, and can restore near-normal function in nearly sixty days![15]

It is truly miraculous that without thought, acknowledgement, or even effort, our bodies improve themselves every second of every day. Much like the other deeply parallel verses of the Bible, "our bodies are temples," they are unlike anything else in the universe. Even if we try to consciously deny God's existence, our very own existence glorifies Him. Things have changed since the beginning of creation, cellular replication is limited, but the design implementation is still there and is helpful for healing.

Another example of our eternal engineering is that our bodies once had—and still have—the ability to synthesize many of our own vitamins. We, or rather the bacteria in our intestines, synthesize vitamins K1 and K2, necessary ingredients for blood clotting, strengthening bones, and other biological processes. Our digestive system also produces intrinsic factors that allow for the absorption of other vital cofactors, particularly vitamin B12. We also synthesize choline and inositol, two important brain vitamins, in our livers. We also used to be able to synthesize our own vitamin C, but those genes have been switched off. (It is discussed further in the next chapter.) Many of these processes have been slowed down or turned off completely, but they still demonstrate God's original intent for our lives.

Our bodies also manufacture vitamin D from the cholesterol in our skin when exposed to the sun. Malachi 4:2 (ESV) says, "But for you who fear my name, the sun of righteousness shall rise with healing in its wings." Note the double metaphor of the word *sun*: literal sunlight provides physical healing, and the Son of God provides spiritual healing. Vitamin D behaves much like a hormone: it boosts our long-term immune systems, affects our brain chemistry, improves our absorption of calcium, and so on.

Most importantly, God designed vitamin D to repair DNA. Our DNA is loaded with nuclear vitamin D receptors (NR1I1 - nuclear receptor subfamily 1, group I, member 1) that controls gene expression. In other words, vitamin D heals and protects DNA.

Our ability to synthesize some of our own vitamins, to regenerate our own cells, and to repair our own DNA are all scientific examples of how we were created by God and designed to live forever. When it comes to our health, God teaches us through the Bible how to manage our foods, environment, and stress in an optimized way. His design is to support the intrinsic self-healing systems in our bodies so we can have natural longevity and innate health.

THE FALL

According to the Bible, God created the universe to be in perfect harmony with Him. People were intended to live in a state of perfect utopia with God forever. However, mankind quickly took advantage of the freedom God gave and rebelled against Him. They chose to "become like God" (Genesis 3:5–7) instead of being subservient to God. After that rebellion, God cursed mankind, His environment, and ultimately the state of the universe itself, thus ending mankind's ability to live forever.

This biblical worldview is in agreement with science through the second law of thermodynamics, or entropy, the gradual decline in available energy in any system. For example, the sun and stars are slowly dying. Someday they will use up all available energy, suffer a heat death, and collapse upon themselves. Earth's rotation is gradually slowing down. The oceans are slowly becoming more acidic. Cars break down over time, houses eventually collapse, gardens get overgrown, and sadly people age.

The Bible teaches that mankind would have to sweat to eat and fight against "thorns and thistles" in order to cultivate crops. It has been observed from amber (fossilized sap from extinct trees) that the oxygen density of the atmosphere is lower today than it used to be. Also the earth is permanently losing certain molecules, such as helium, into space and will one day run out.

People are also hostile to each other and more destructive to the planet than designed by God. Stephen Hawking, the world's most adamant atheist and evolutionist, believed that humanity would not survive another two hundred years due to its destructive patterns, which is ironic since he believed that humans are the most advanced evolutionary species. This proclamation comes from the scientific fact that 52 percent of the earth's wildlife has been lost in the past forty years due to human industrial behavior.[16]

In Genesis 3, God also cursed mankind's health. Our genetic makeup was changed to limit immortality. Though our bodies were originally designed to heal naturally forever via cellular regeneration, after the events of Genesis 3, God put a limit on that process. The limit, or the "Hayflick limit," was named for the man who discovered it in 1961.

At that time, Leonard Hayflick discovered that there is a piece of DNA at the end of each chromosome of every cell, the telomere, which gets progressively shorter every time the cell duplicates. As a result, the sequence shortens over time until the cell can no longer replicate itself and it permanently dies. According to research, the life span of each cell is directly related to the length of its telomere, and the length of the telomere is directly related to aging, mortality, and age-related diseases.[17]

Scientists have been studying the telomere since its discovery and have concluded that the average maximum life span of the human body, based on telomere length, is roughly 120 years. The irony, of course, is that God told us centuries ago in Genesis 6:3 (NIV), "My Spirit shall not abide in man forever, for he is flesh: the days (of man) shall be 120 years." The genetic potential for a human being is capped at roughly 120 years.

It is important to note that the telomere is extremely susceptible to oxidative stress. So in our current state of living, antioxidants, which are found naturally in God's diet, are extremely important for protecting the life span of the cell and its ability to replicate.

A second genetic change that occurred was disabling the gene that controls our ability to synthesize vitamin C, one of our most powerful antioxidant and anti-aging vitamins. In a recent study of aging disorders, vitamin C was the most effective of numerous compounds in lengthening telomeres. It also protects our brains, hearts, blood vessels, skin, and tendons. It decreases pain levels for all pathologies, helps regulate blood sugar, and fights toxins and viruses. In fact, it is used in every single system in the body. The most important characteristic of vitamin C is that it protects us from our own cellular metabolism. It recycles the waste products that occur in our cells when we use energy—when we move around, work, sleep, breathe, or do anything.

It also increases and enhances the other antioxidants in the cell, such as glutathione and vitamin E, which further compounds its anti-aging properties.[18] Recycling these protective molecules is like having a car that would take its own smog and turn it into fuel for the car. It would never need a tune-up because it would be self-maintaining and non-polluting.

In the beginning, God designed us to produce our own vitamin C. In our genetic code, we have the blueprints to create vitamin C from sugar. However, our DNA has been rewired, and the process necessary to create vitamin C has been turned off. In the equation, the gene that controls the final chemical, a substrate, has been disabled. This chemical is known as gulonolactone oxidase, and its gene (chromosome 8p21) has been appropriately labeled GULO.

Gulonolactone oxidase attaches an oxygen molecule to a type of sugar molecule (L-xylo-hex-3-gulonolactone), which converts it to ascorbic acid, or vitamin C. Without gulonolactone oxidase, it is impossible for us to make vitamin C, and we are forced to try to consume it through our diet. We are one of the few creatures on the planet who cannot complete this equation.

Vitamin C Equation:

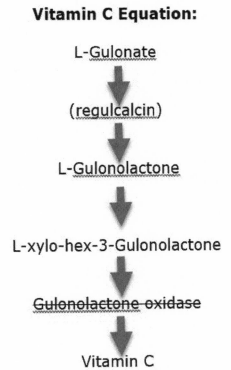

L-Gulonate

⬇

(regulcalcin)

⬇

L-Gulonolactone

⬇

L-xylo-hex-3-Gulonolactone

⬇

~~Gulonolactone oxidase~~

⬇

Vitamin C

This gene malfunction is a great argument for intelligent design. If we evolved, why would we evolve and then disable the gene that creates vitamin C? That is not a beneficial mutation in any way. We desperately need that GULO gene for our health and an increased life span. I believe this gene is disabled because the science of genetics aligns perfectly with the Bible: God created us with perfect genes, but due to sin, we are now cursed with imperfect DNA. Our genetics are not improving with time but instead are declining.

Genetic science illuminates what was written in Genesis 2:17 of the Bible: מֹות תָּמֽוּת. Notice how some of the letters repeat themselves in the two words. The literal translation of the Hebrew text is "dying you shall die," using a future perfect tense of the verb. It indicates an action that has started but not yet been completed, as opposed to the immediate future tense of "you will die today."

This verse teaches that the process has started but not yet come to full fruition. Our genetics show God's grace toward mankind by giving people the opportunity for life, love, children, and the experience of knowing God. Yet our genetics are a reminder that mankind rejected God, became cursed, and desperately need forgiveness and salvation from Him.

In summary, we were designed to live forever but are no longer able to do so. However, we have not yet begun to tap into the full genetic potential as human beings that God has designed us for. We were created in God's image as the most superior creatures on earth, designed to most supremely reflect our God and Creator. And most importantly, He has provided us with the Bible to provide insight on how to express our full potential for our own glory and His, and if we apply His principles, He promises a long, healthy, disease-free, and blessed life. The entirety of the rest of the book will focus on the principles that are propagated in the Bible and backed by science in order to bring to light the incredible journey of health that God designed and promised for us to enjoy.

EMOTIONAL HEALTH

One of the most amazing features of human nature is the ability to synthesize relationships, emotions, connections, and a sense of self, our spiritual nature. All these things are orchestrated through our brain. Even after centuries of studying, utilizing all modern technology, and accumulating all knowledge, we still do not understand most of how the brain works, especially how it connects us to the supernatural. The human brain is by far the most complex structure in the entire universe.

Physically, a single human brain has more neuronal connections than the entire World Wide Web. Each nerve cell is more complex than a NASA space shuttle. It saves every memory from every moment of our lives and can store at least 100 trillion units of data (as far as we can measure with modern technology), including memories, emotional responses, ideas, abstracts, theories, and more. It can spontaneously create new ideas out of literally almost anything. And unlike any other species on the planet, the human brain contains an overtly complex structure called the prefrontal cortex, which governs morality, decision making, reasoning, and empathy. It creates personality and is the part of the brain that makes us "human."

No other animal contains that portion of the brain. It is highly organized and serves a higher function than all other lobes of the brain. It provides within all humans everywhere a moral compass, a sense of empathy, and the profound state of self-awareness. Science from multiple fields demonstrates that people contain a sense of morality and self-awareness that no other creature in the universe shares. Sociologists agree that no matter what one's background, race, creed, or environment is, all human behavior demonstrates a universal moral code. For example, no culture, past or present, has ever endorsed stabbing someone in the back who has helped you or saved your life. No culture has ever championed as courageous the one who ran from battle or abandoned his family or comrades in a time of crisis.

Neurophysiologists have demonstrated through MRI that this portion of the human brain, the prefrontal cortex, is highly active when making serious moral or self-awareness decisions. No other creature's brain has this type of complexity. Even the world's fastest supercomputers cannot replicate the processing power of the human brain. It alone has the ability for introspection, empathy, meditation, discerning morality, and so forth.

We have another portion of our brain, the temporal lobe, where religiosity, elitism, entitlement, and temper tantrums (the opposite of self-awareness) arise. The prefrontal cortex inhibits or dampens the temporal lobe so we are less irrational, temperamental, and self-centered and more rational about misguided religiousness.

Our brains, when working in totality, allow us to feel God intensely and emotionally and allow us to engage and participate with Him in our lives pragmatically. That is why the Bible tells us to "be transformed by the renewing of our mind" (Romans 12:2 NIV) because our whole brain, not just certain lobes, must be renewed. Otherwise we become mentally imbalanced. This explains the seemingly confusing paradox of "saved by grace alone" from Ephesians 2:8 (ESV) and "faith by itself, if it does not have works, is dead" from James 2:17 (ESV).

The Bible is not teaching that faith is purely emotional, nor works-based actions. The Bible is compelling us, in congruence with the science of neurology, to allow the grace of God to permeate all lobes of our brain so God's love affects our thoughts and emotions and compels our behavior. We are more unique than anything else on the planet because we have the ability to engage with our Creator and to others through the different lobes of the brain. We can project our thoughts and ideas beyond primitive instincts.

Therefore, the human brain allows us to experience true love that no other species on the planet can experience. It is a sacrificial love, and it is extremely healthy for us to develop. With lust, the animalistic, primitive portions of the brain light up on brain scans (lobes of the brain that exist in all instinctual creatures on the earth). However, in healthy, long-term human relationships, all aspects of the brain, including the prefrontal cortex, are being used.

Most importantly, as it pertains to our health, when someone who loves another person touches that individual, healing chemicals known as pheromones, as well as specific hormones and neurotransmitters, are produced throughout the body to stimulate healing and provide both people with a heightened sense of well-being. The deeper the love, the stronger the chemical output.

For example, newborn babies who lay on their mother's chests will harmonize with their mother so efficiently that they synchronize their heart rhythm to their mothers. In the Bible, we are told that Jesus is love (John 4:16), which explains very accurately the science behind how if He touched someone (or someone touched Him), that person would be instantly healed of all disease. This is also why the two greatest commandments were "Love the Lord your God with all your heart, with all your soul, and with all your mind" and "Love your neighbor as yourself" because we have the ability to affect our health in a dramatic way by developing compassion and empathy with others.

Again, He is commanding that we allow God's love to permeate all lobes of our brain, to receive healing from it, and then to share this love and its healing ability with the others. This is an amazing example of how we were created in God's likeness, with a purpose to love, a timeline to live forever, and an ability to change the physiology of ourselves and everyone around us.

The Bible's message of hope is that "everyone who calls on the name of the LORD will be saved" (Romans 10:13 NLT). Why would Jesus spend a vast majority of his ministry on earth performing miracles? He sought to "Heal the brokenhearted, preach deliverance to the captives, and recovery of sight to the blind" (Luke 4:18 KJV). The power of God is the most important aspect to all healing, and it occurs on a physical and spiritual level.

Ultimately we must know and believe that God created us for life and we have been designed from the beginning to be eternally healthy. There are so many aspects to our emotional health that are discussed in the Bible at length that I always recommend licensed Christian professionals for everyone because the implications of our emotional health are both serious and consequential to our lives.

PHYSICAL HEALTH

The practical application of the Bible is to align our diet and lifestyle with God's original plan. Dieting and lifestyle choices are two of the largest swinging fads in America. There are many different, seemingly conflicting, opinions about what is healthy. There are so many books, blogs, videos, and television shows that the subject can become quite confusing. In this era of post-information, it is not a lack of information that hinders people, but an overwhelming and baffling amount of it.

Consider all the people you know who have gone on a diet and not lost weight, lost weight only to gain it back again later, or even had bad side effects of the diet itself. Also consider how the US government has constantly changed its recommendations for the standard diet over the past hundred years. The USDA food guides have changed from five food groups in 1916 to twelve in the 1930s, four in the 1950s and 1960s, and now six in the food pyramid. Combine that with the plethora of conflicting consumer information about health and it is no wonder everyone is confused!

One of the names of Satan in the Bible is the "prince of the power of air" (Ephesians 2:1–3), meaning he is supreme at lying and spreading propaganda. Many of the consumer messages about health are conflicting, misleading, or downright inaccurate. Many diet plans are short-term fads that do not work long term or are designed to sell books, products, or subscriptions.

In contrast, the Bible's recommendations have never changed, contradicted themselves, or been attached to a hidden monetary agenda, despite what some people would accuse, and have always been in agreement with what science tells us about our bodies, physiology, and inherent design for digestion and assimilation of nutrients. Therefore, for the remainder of this book, we are going to extract the dietary truths found in the Bible and apply them to the truths found in science in order to formulate the healthiest possible dietary choices for our lives. The goal is to help maximize our genetic potential for God's glory. After all, Jesus came so we could "have life, and have it abundantly" (John 10:10 ESV).

Here is a brief recap of what we know about ourselves, our starting point for health, and the philosophical context in which we will pursue the proper diet, based on science and biblical principles:

- Our bodies are intimately conjoined with our spirits and our souls.
- Our bodies were designed to live forever, but no longer do so.
- Our bodies heal and repair by constantly replacing old dying cells with new healthy cells.
- Our bodies are genetically programmed for cellular replication for around 120 years.
- Our bodies synthesize some of our vital nutrients, like vitamin D and K, but must obtain the others through food sources, like vitamin C.
- Our environment has been cursed and no longer works for us without our own cultivation.

The key to physical health is creating harmony in the body by balancing its structure, function, and chemistry. Medically known as "homeostasis," it is achieved through diet and lifestyle. Our dietary nutrients are obtained by consuming foods and drinks. The three major types of nutrients—proteins, fats, and carbohydrates—are called macros because they are required in large quantities. Most people need equal portions of each, although various conditions might require a shift to favor one category over another.

There are nutrients known as "micros" or "micronutrients," which are only needed in trace amounts but are still absolutely necessary for life. There are other aspects to physical health, also discussed in the Bible, that have to do with our interaction with the environment: food preparation, sanitation, cultivation of the environment, and so forth. These are all necessary for proper health because without them, we could not survive physically. Fortunately God provides all of the tools on earth and the knowledge in the Bible. We will discuss each of these major points in the following chapters. For even more information, you can check out our website, a portal for up-to-date information on biblical health, diet, lifestyle, meal plans, recipes, and so on: http://www.DesignerDiet.org or http://www.DrMelot.com.

PROTEIN

Discovered in 1838, protein has since become the most emphasized unit of nutrition in the Western world. Proteins are macromolecules, or large molecules, that are most commonly recognized as the building blocks for our bodies. They are converted into the structural pieces used to build muscle, bone, cellular components, and so on. Not only that, but they are also involved in almost every other cellular process in the body. For example, proteins are used to transport components (e.g., other nutrients) around cells. Proteins are used to control tissue fluid levels via osmosis, the flow of water from less dense to denser areas.

Proteins are used to regulate blood pH, keeping our bodies from becoming fatally acidic or basic. Proteins can also be used as enzymes, which accelerate chemical reactions in the body. Proteins can even be burned for energy as a last resort if the body does not have any available carbs or fat. There are an abundance of other uses for proteins as well, and they are one of the most important macronutrients.

Proteins can be broken down into smaller units of nutrition called amino acids. Different amino acids have distinct roles in the body, and as a result, not all proteins can be broken down and used for the same purposes. This is significant to know because not all dietary protein sources contain all of the amino acids, and not having a full spectrum of bioavailable amino acids can be dangerous, although this is very rare in Western diets. Our bodies can synthesize some amino acids, but there are a few amino acids that can only be obtained through our diet, which are called essential amino acids. Therefore, even a seemingly high protein diet can be lacking in one or more essential amino acids if we are not deliberate about our protein intake. Here is a list of the essential amino acids:

Histidine	Isoleucine	Leucine
Lysine	Methionine	Phenylalanine
Threonine	Tryptophan	Valine

Dietary sources of protein are quite abundant, so the real discretion is to determine which foods have the best bioavailability of the necessary amino acids. God's original design was for us to eat exclusively from the plant kingdom. "Behold, I have given you every plant yielding seed that is on the face of all the earth, and every tree with seed in its fruit. You shall have them for food" (Genesis 1:29 ESV). And contrary to popular myth, you absolutely can obtain the entire spectrum of essential amino acids from the plant kingdom. The advantage of protein from plants is that it is cleaner than animal sources (no toxins) and easier to digest than protein from meat sources. A lot of plant protein sources even exceed meat protein sources for certain amino acids (e.g., spirulina, a seaweed that contains more threonine than meat). Furthermore, plant proteins are coupled with other quality ingredients to assist in other biochemical reactions in the body (e.g., phytonutrients, vitamins, minerals, etc.).

In addition, studies show that plant-based diets significantly lower a person's risk of heart disease, cancer, stroke, and diabetes (the top four causes of death in the United States).

Here is a table of some of the best sources of amino acids in the plant kingdom for each essential amino acid:

Histidine	Buckwheat, Beans, Cantaloupe, Cauliflower, Chia Seeds, Corn, Hemp Seeds, Legumes, Potatoes, Rice, Rye, Seaweed, Wheat
Isoleucine	Almonds, Apples, Beans, Blueberries, Brown Rice, Cabbage, Cashews, Chia Seeds, Cranberries, Hemp Seeds, Kiwis, Lentils, Oats, Pumpkin (and Seeds), Quinoa, Rye, Sesame Seeds, Soy, Spinach, Sunflower Seeds
Leucine	Apples, Avocados, Bananas, Blueberries, Dates, Figs, Kidney Beans, Olives, Peas, Pumpkin, Raisins, Rice, Seaweed, Sesame Seeds, Soy, Sunflower Seeds, Turnips (and Turnip Greens), Watercress

Lysine	Almonds, Avocado, Beans, Cashews, Chia Seeds, Chickpeas, Hemp Seeds, Legumes, Lentils, Parsley, Soy, Spirulina, Watercress
Methionine	Beans, Brazil Nuts, Cacao, Chia Seeds, Figs, Hemp Seeds, Legumes, Oats, Onions, Raisins, Seaweed, Sunflower Seeds, Wheat, Whole Grain Rice
Phenylalanine	Almonds, Avocados, Beans, Berries, Figs, Leafy Greens, Olives, Quinoa, Peanuts, Pumpkin, Raisins, Rice, Seaweed, Seeds, Spirulina
Threonine	Almonds, Avocados, Chia Seeds, Figs, Hemp Seeds, Leafy Greens, Pumpkin, Quinoa, Raisins, Sesame Seeds, Soy, Spirulina, Sprouted Grains, Sunflower Seeds, Watercress
Tryptophan	Apples, Asparagus, Avocados, Bananas, Beans, Beets, Carrots, Celery, Chia Seeds, Chickpeas, Figs, Hemp Seeds, Leafy Greens, Lentils, Lettuces, Mushrooms, Oats, Onions, Oranges, Parsley, Peas, Peppers, Pumpkins, Quinoa, Seaweed, Soy, Spinach, Sweet Potatoes, Watercress, Winter Squash
Valine	Apples, Apricots, Avocado, Beans, Blueberries, Broccoli, Chia Seeds, Cranberries, Figs, Hemp Seeds, Legumes, Oranges, Peanuts, Sesame Seeds, Soy, Spinach, Sprouted Grains

Here is a table of the plants and plant combinations that contain all of the amino acids:

Quinoa	Hemp Seeds
Buckwheat	Chia Seeds
Hummus and Pita Bread	Rice and Beans
Spirulina	Ezekiel Bread

Certain amino acids can even be used to drive biochemical pathways. This is called "targeted amino acid therapy," in which high doses of very specific amino acids are used to push biochemical pathways in order to stimulate a medicinal, or healing, effect on the body. For example, the amino acid 5-HTP or 5-Hydroxytryptophan is a precursor for serotonin, the feel-good neurotransmitter.

Therefore, if you are deficient in serotonin, excess 5-HTP from your diet can help increase the production of serotonin. In fact, scientific studies have been performed on these theories and have demonstrated that 5-HTP has been shown to be more effective than antidepressant medicine for treating mild depression and anxiety.[19]

Hippocrates once said, "Let thy food be thy medicine and let thy medicine be thy food," and this is a great example of that. If you are suffering from some of these brain chemistry imbalances, try eating one cup of cashews daily, which will contain a therapeutic dose of 5-HTP, along with B vitamins and anti-inflammatory fats, all of which are extremely beneficial for balancing brain chemistry.

This is an example of how God's food is designed specifically for our health. It helps prevent disease and restore natural health with no side effects. In the appendix, I have listed specific foods to be eaten in higher concentrations for various common health problems found in the United States population, not as a singular healing modality but in order to strongly counteract nutritional deficiencies and bring homeostasis or balance back to the body.

Even though God's original design was to eat exclusively from the plant kingdom, He later approved of an expanded dietary plan for humans to include some meat. "Every moving thing that lives shall be food for you. And as I gave you the green plants, I give you everything" (Genesis 9:3 ESV).

In other words, it's not the end of the world if you eat meat, and it does have some benefits, but it simply isn't as beneficial as plant protein for long-term healthiness. An epidemiological study performed by professors at USC concluded that eating a diet high in animal protein during the Middle Ages increased chance of cancer by four times.[20]

Paul clarifies the concept of Old Testament law with regard to Christians in 1 Corinthians 10:23 (ESV). "'All things are lawful,' but not all things are helpful. 'All things are lawful,' but not all things build up." In other words, we can eat whatever we want, but certain foods are healthier for our bodies than other foods. The Bible goes into specific details about these foods in Leviticus when God was providing the Israelites with a more comprehensive dietary plan.

These are the living things that you may eat among all the animals that are on the earth: Whatever parts the hoof and is cloven-footed and chews the cud, among the animals, you may eat. Nevertheless, among those that chew the cud or part the hoof, you shall not eat these: The camel, because it chews the cud but does not part the hoof, is unclean to you. And the rock badger, because it chews the cud but does not part the hoof, is unclean to you. And the hare, because it chews the cud but does not part the hoof, is unclean to you. And the pig, because it parts the hoof and is cloven-footed but does not chew the cud, is unclean to you. You shall not eat any of their flesh, and you shall not touch their carcasses; they are unclean to you.

These you may eat, of all that are in the waters. Everything in the waters that has fins and scales, whether in the seas or in the rivers, you may eat. But anything in the seas or the rivers that does not have fins and scales, of the swarming creatures in the waters and of the living creatures that are in the waters, is detestable to you. You shall regard them as detestable; you shall not eat any of their flesh, and you shall detest their carcasses. Everything in the waters that does not have fins and scales is detestable to you.

And these you shall detest among the birds; they shall not be eaten; they are detestable: the eagle, the bearded vulture, the black vulture, the kite, the falcon of any kind, every raven of any kind, the ostrich, the nighthawk, the sea gull, the hawk of any kind, the little owl, the cormorant, the short-eared owl, the barn owl, the tawny owl, the carrion vulture, the stork, the heron of any kind, the hoopoe, and the bat. (Leviticus 11:3–19 ESV)

These verses are describing certain animal protein sources that are healthy (clean) and some that are not. Interestingly, despite being seemingly wordy, these laws are congruent with what science tells us about health and nutrition. For example, God tells us not to eat pig meat, and we now know that pork has a high concentration of arachidonic acid, a type of fat that is inflammatory to the body and creates disease processes. In fact, epidemiological studies routinely demonstrate that societies that consume more pork have more cases of cancer and other inflammatory diseases.

According to the Bible, there is a hierarchy of good and bad meat sources, listed according to the way in which they classified animals in their day (by observable features such as "chewing cud" or "split hoof"). They also had a systematic way to procure the meat, which, to this day, is so healthy that modern kosher meat processing facilities aren't regulated by the USFDA because they are so far beyond the minimum requirements set by our government for cleanliness.

I have reorganized the information into an easier classification system (without changing the content). The most common meats are listed in the chart in four categories: good, better, best, and "do not eat." The best meats have the least amount of inflammatory properties of animal protein. They also contain the highest concentration of healthy fats, which I will discuss in the next chapter. This is not an exhaustive list, but hopefully a thorough guide to navigate through the common meats eaten around the world:

Good	Cow, Deer, Ox, Sheep, Goat, Gazelle, Antelope, Bison
Better	Chicken, Turkey, Goose, Duck
Best	*Eggs, Non-Bottom–Feeding Fish with Scales and Fins (Salmon, Tuna, Halibut, Snapper, etc.)
Do Not Eat	Land Animals: Rabbit, Squirrel, Hyrax (and Other Rodents), Cat, Dog, Wolf, Bear, Horse, Pig, Camel, Rhino
	Flying Animals: Eagle, Owl, Swan, Pelican, Vulture, Stork, Bat
	Marine Animals: Crustaceans (Lobster, Crab, Shrimp), Catfish, Mollusks, Shellfish, Eel, Sea Cucumbers, Jellyfish, Dolphin, Whale, Alligator, Crocodile, Sea Turtle, Sea Snake, Bottom-Feeding Fish, Amphibians
	None except Locust, Beetle, Cricket, Grasshopper

*Eggs contain the full spectrum of amino acids, which make them a very good source of protein. However, they are the second-most common food allergy in the United States (2 percent of the population). If you struggle with allergic conditions such as eczema, you should seriously consider omitting eggs from your diet or being tested for food allergies.

The reason why the Bible lists "chewing cud" as a requirement for acceptable meat is because those animals have multiple stomach chambers and are able to process nutrients more efficiently, thus passing those benefits to us. In addition, this type of stomach mechanism (the opposite of what humans have) requires less gut bacteria for the digestive process, which limits our exposure to the possibility of ingesting bad bacteria and becoming sick. The unclean animals, the ones with single stomach chambers (monogastric fermenters), rely on bacteria to fully break down food particles. These bacteria create phytanic acid when it digests animal protein, which is highly inflammatory. (This is why humans aren't as adept at consuming meat.) If we eat meat and produce phytanic acid from a source that is already rich in phytanic acid, we develop an immune response after eating that meal, which is why plant-based diets are so beneficial for counteracting autoimmune diseases.

That is why the Bible specifically recommends against eating animals that do not "chew their cud." As an aside, Oxford performed a study on this and demonstrated that people who were on a typical American diet had 6.7 times higher concentration of phytanic acid in their bloodstreams than vegans.[21]

As a result, our red meat selection is quite limited: cattle, goats, sheep, bison, deer, and antelope. The main advantage of consuming these red meats are their concentration of the amino acids L-leucine, L-isoleucine, L-valine, and L-arginine, which are good for building muscle mass and increasing blood flow into the muscles. They should be utilized as weight gainers for people who want or need to increase muscle mass.

With regard to ocean animals, the scientific reason why bottom-dwelling fish and crustaceans are not on the acceptable list is that they feed off the excrement from other water animals. This causes them to be more susceptible to ingesting toxins and excreting parasites. In fact, one article suggested that possibly 85 percent of Americans are unknowingly infected by parasites in their bowels, and the Centers for Disease Control and Prevention (CDC) published that, definitively, 14 percent of Americans do test positive for parasites. Since parasites only come from "dirty" meat sources, this is another reminder to try to stick to clean meats as much as possible.

Fish with scales and fins are considered clean according to the Bible. They also happen to be the absolute best source of animal-based protein available. They are loaded with antioxidants (from diets high in green algae), full-spectrum minerals (from the waters), and healthy fats (which counteract inflammatory fats). Fortunately, there are over 20,000 species of acceptable fish, with new ones being discovered every year. These fish are great for the brain, skin, hair, nails, and other parts of the body, and both the dietary and scientific communities highly recommend them for their health benefits.

The last protein source to discuss is birds. Scavenger birds are unacceptable because they have lots of environmental toxins in their bodies. Non-scavenger birds are an excellent source of protein though. They are generally very lean, do not create toxic metabolites when digested, and contain a full amino acid profile (all of the amino acids).

The biggest advantage of bird meat, specifically turkey, is that it has a much higher concentration of tryptophan than other animal proteins, which makes it beneficial in conjunction with FDA-approved treatments for naturally balancing neurotransmitters (brain chemicals) in conditions such as depression, anxiety, sleeplessness, and so on. It is important to note that protein from the bird kingdom does not have the same anti-inflammatory properties as plant or fish protein, so they are considered a mid-tier protein source.

So how much total protein do we need to eat daily? Various sources will recommend between 10 and 35 percent of our food intake. A better way to calculate is to utilize your current size and weight. You need approximately 0.36 grams per pound of body weight to maintain muscle weight. Anything less than that will cause you to burn your own muscle to recycle the amino acids. This is not the kind of weight loss you want to attain. If you are trying to gain muscle mass, you need up to one gram of protein per pound of body weight. Here are the formulas written out for a calculator:

Maintenance
Your Weight = x 0.36 = _____g
Grams of protein per day

Muscle Growth
Your Weight = ___x 1 = _____g
Grams of protein per day

Here is a chart of common clean protein sources and the amount of protein that they contain:

Lentils (1 cup)	18 grams
Split Green Peas (1 cup)	8 grams
Hemp Seeds (3 tablespoons)	10 grams
Chia Seeds (2 tablespoons)	4 grams
Quinoa (1/2 cup)	8 grams
Spirulina (2 tablespoons)	8 grams
Seeds (Sunflower, etc.) (1/4 cup)	7–9 grams
Nuts (1/4 cup)	7–9 grams
Beans (1 cup)	Approximately 15 grams
Peanut Butter (2 tablespoons)	8 grams
Greek Yogurt (8 ounces)	23 grams
Cottage Cheese (1/2 cup)	14 grams
Eggs (1 large)	6 grams
Steak (3 ounces)	23 grams
Ground Beef (85 percent lean) (3 ounces)	22 grams
Chicken (3 ounces)	21 grams
Turkey (3 ounces)	18 grams
Duck (3 ounces)	16 grams
Tuna (3 ounces)	25 grams
Halibut (3 ounces)	23 grams
Salmon (3 ounces)	23 grams

Ultimately, the goal is to eat enough protein to fuel your body; grow healthy, lean muscle; and contribute to the long-term health of your system. The best way to do this is to follow the Bible's guidelines, perform scientific research, and seek out the best protein sources available. This should consist primarily of plant proteins, clean fish, non-scavenging birds, and lean, clean, grass-fed land animals with minimal processing.

FAT

Fat is the third of the three macronutrients—fat, protein, and carbohydrates—which means it is a type of food that is essential to our health. For instance, our bodies use fat in the following ways: the majority of our brains are made up of fat (over 60 percent), the lining of our cells are made of fat, all of our steroid hormones are created from fat, we burn fat for energy, we store future energy in fat, and we displace toxins in fat if we cannot expel them. There are many other processes in the body that use fat, so suffice it to say, we must have fat in our diet to be healthy.

Unfortunately there are many different types of fats. Some are extremely healthy; others are extremely unhealthy. Even good fat can become unhealthy through food processing, age, heat, or other factors. It is imperative to be able to distinguish good fats from the bad. Most Americans have fat metabolism problems that could be improved by utilizing the correct types of fat. The great news is that the body will replace unhealthy fats with healthy ones when given the opportunity. In other words, introducing healthy fat in the diet can reverse unhealthy fat metabolism.

Fats are made up of long chains of carbon molecules known as fatty acids. They are called "acids" because the long chains have a slightly acidic pH. The fats are classified by the way in which the carbon molecules are attached to each other. Saturated fats have a single bond between the carbon molecules with hydrogen molecules attached to them. The length can vary depending upon the type of fat, and the ends can have other structures attached to them, but here is the basic structure.

SATURATED FAT

Most saturated fats are not healthy for our bodies and are found in excess in the forbidden foods as prescribed by the Bible. "Do not eat any fat of cattle, sheep, or goats" (Leviticus 7:23 NIV). The reason is that these fats contain chains that are very long, even up to ten times longer than my picture, so they do not function well in the body. They clog up arteries and so forth. Also there are not clear breakpoints in the chains so when we break them apart to try to use them, our bodies end up with oxidative fragments everywhere.

That means these fragments are the opposite of an antioxidant. They are very reactive to other molecules in the cells. They crash around and break cellular components, which causes havoc on the other structures and functions in the body. Medical research has demonstrated that excess saturated fats increase the risk of type 2 diabetes, insulin resistance, obesity, atherosclerosis, and other chronic degenerative diseases. While there are a few exceptions, saturated fats should generally not be the primary source of fat in our diets.

Unsaturated fats are different because they have double bonds between the carbon molecules at specific sequences. This gives them an angled shape. It also gives them easy break points so that when we metabolize them, we create specific medium-chain fatty acids that are not too big, not oxidative in nature, and not damaging to our cells.

UNSATURATED FATS

Because of these properties, the medium-chain fatty acids from unsaturated fats are very stable. They are great sources of energy for our body because they can be rapidly absorbed into the bloodstream and quickly metabolized. For this reason, they are more often burned for fuel rather than stored as fat. Therefore, they actually improve our metabolism. This is the opposite of long-chain saturated fats, which slow our metabolism, are not easily digested, and are generally converted to storage fat in our bodies.

Unsaturated fats are also ideal for building fat-based components such as cell walls and brain tissue. All of these properties make unsaturated fats the best type of fat for our bodies. They should be the main type of fat that we consume. In fact, thousands of scientific studies demonstrate the medicinal, or healing, effects that unsaturated fats have on the body. Here are a few:

- Reduces risk of all-cause mortality in 4,500 men with prostate cancer[22]
- Has an inverse relationship to breast cancer risk[23]
- Improves diabetes risk factors[24]
- Helps control blood sugar in people with type 2 diabetes[25]
- Reduces inflammation (C-reactive protein) in the body[26]
- Reduces risk of stroke[27]
- Reduces risk of Alzheimer's disease[28]
- Reduces bad fats in the body[29]
- Reduces belly fat[30]

The list could go on for pages because there are literally thousands of medical articles covering every organ and system in the body that show how beneficial unsaturated fats are for our health. These are the type of fats that God designed for us to eat, and their benefits are wide-ranging and powerful.

The primary source for unsaturated fats is from the plant kingdom. They are found in the highest quantities in the nuts, seeds, and nut oils from plants. Of course, every other part of the plant also contains unsaturated fats: the leaves, stems, fruits, and flowers. Many fruits, such as avocadoes, contain high amounts of unsaturated fats. Unsaturated fats are also found in fish and, to a lesser extent, herbivores.

The last type of fats, trans fats, are unsaturated fats that synthetic processes force into saturation. They appear in processed foods as "partially hydrogenated oils." Food production companies choose them because they are cheap to produce, have a long shelf life, taste good, and can be reusable many times in deep fryers. Unfortunately, trans fats are very unhealthy for our bodies. They are not normal or natural in any way, shape, or form, and as such, our bodies do not metabolize them without consequences. They are not specifically mentioned in the Bible because, at the time, humans had not invented them yet.

However, there are several allusions to trans fats when the Bible discusses the adulteration of our food supply in Leviticus 19:19 and Deuteronomy 22:9–11. It says not to mix two types of plant seeds in the same field, two types of cattle in the same herd, or even to mix animal and plant threads (linen and wool) together in a garment. In other words, don't adulterate our food sources because they will no longer be natural and will no longer be the best type of food for our body.

Trans fats are a perfect example of this. They are bad for our health and accelerate our body's degeneration in every way possible, and they do not create health in any pathway in our body. They should be avoided if at all possible, under all circumstances.

Interestingly, thousands of years before we knew all about the biochemistry of fat, the Bible explained very clearly which fats were good and which were bad. Not surprisingly, the Bible perfectly delineates what we now know about healthy and unhealthy fats based on nutritional science. It teaches specific principles that will dramatically improve our health in the area of fat intake and metabolism.

The Bible tells us first and foremost to eat nuts, seeds, and plants. In fact, it is God's first nutritional command. "I have given you every plant yielding seed that is on the face of all the earth, and every tree with seed in its fruit. You shall have them for food" (Genesis 1:29 ESV). This is because plants are the perfect food for us. They contain the perfect ratio of carbohydrates, fats, and protein; the fats are entirely monounsaturated fats, the most important type for our bodies.

The wording of that Bible verse appears somewhat strange when translated to English, but it is clear that God is directly instructing people to also eat the seeds and nuts along with the meat of the plants. This is because the portion of the plant with the highest density of fats is actually the seeds and nuts. We now know that seeds and nuts are the absolute best sources of fat for our bodies because they exclusively contain monounsaturated fat, the best type of fat for our bodies. The stems, leaves, fruit, and other parts of the plant also contain fat, just to a lesser degree than the seeds.

Therefore, you can also get monounsaturated fats from fruits such as avocados. Diets rich in these foods and fats have been shown to provide an enormous health benefit for our bodies. They reduce the risk of heart disease, stroke, type 2 diabetes, and other chronic diseases. Monounsaturated fats from the plant kingdom are absolutely imperative to our diets in order to have the health that God designed for us and to live the life that God designed for us to live.

The plant kingdom also contains some saturated fats. Yet, interestingly, the saturated fats in the plant kingdom actually do contain health benefits, unlike the saturated fats found in the animal kingdom. Take coconut oil, for example. It contains a medium-chain fatty acid known as lauric acid, which has been shown to increase metabolism (and weight loss), improve the immune system and the elasticity of skin, and so forth. It is also antimicrobial, which means it protects against superficial bacterial, viral, and fungal infections. It also contributes to a healthy brain. There are so many other benefits found in plant-based fats, both saturated and unsaturated, that it would be impossible to list them all here, so suffice it to say, the Bible was in perfect congruence with science when it recommended plant-based fat intake.[31]

The Bible also recommends fish as another fat source. Fish are important because they contain a second type of unsaturated fat known as polyunsaturated fat. Commonly called omega-3s, these polyunsaturated fats are extremely valuable to our bodies. They are antioxidants, which means they protect against free radicals, the molecules that damage our cells. Omega-3s also displace bad fat in fatty tissue, such as the brain or cell walls, which means as you eat them, they will take the place of bad fat and force your body to get rid of the unhealthy fat. Therefore, when you eat them, you create healthier fat structures such as cell walls and brain tissue.

Omega-3s from fish also carry fat-soluble vitamins and are loaded with vital nutrients such as vitamin B12 and D3, among others. Because of all of these reasons, fish should be an important part of our diets. In fact, fish have been an imperative part of the human diet for most of history. They have also been an imperative part of the biblical diet: two of Jesus's disciples were fisherman, several of His miracles involved fish, and the largest miracle and only one recorded in all four gospels, other than the resurrection, was the "feeding of the 5,000," where He fed fish to thousands of people for a day.

Only in recent years have we begun to decrease our fish consumption[32] and increase our shellfish consumption. (And we have observed an increase in illnesses related to consuming dirty meat.) From a biblical and scientific perspective, we need to shift back into eating clean fish, which are fish with scales and fins that are not bottom feeders. Ideally, they should be wild-caught and not farmed. In doing this, we can substantially improve our fat metabolism pathways and our overall healthiness. The type of fat that the Bible explicitly forbids is animal fat. The Bible clearly states in Leviticus 7:23(NASB), "You shall not eat any fat from an oxen, sheep or goats."

As stated above, fats from these sources are unhealthy and should be avoided. The types of fats available to us can get very confusing so here are some graphics to help with fat types, sources, and metabolic pathways:

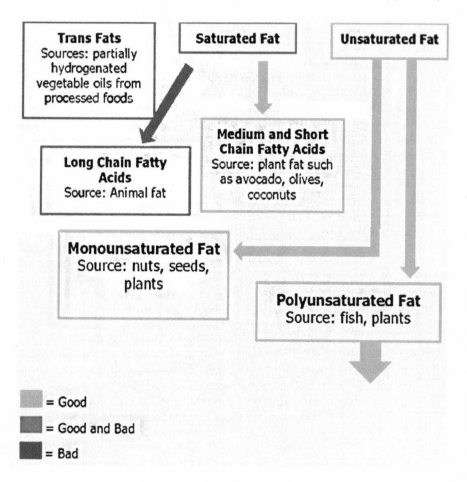

Trans Fats
Sources: partially hydrogenated vegetable oils from processed foods

Saturated Fat

Unsaturated Fat

Long Chain Fatty Acids
Source: Animal fat

Medium and Short Chain Fatty Acids
Source: plant fat such as avocado, olives, coconuts

Monounsaturated Fat
Source: nuts, seeds, plants

Polyunsaturated Fat
Source: fish, plants

= Good

= Good and Bad

= Bad

POLYUNSATURATED FAT METABOLISM

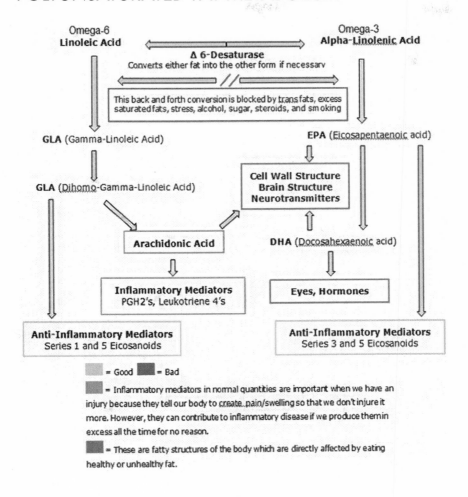

Here are some reference tables for the sources of fats:

Sources of Fat*		
Good	Monounsaturated Fat	Sunflower Oil, Safflower Oil, Hazelnut Oil, Olive Oil, Canola Oil, Avocados, Peanuts, Macadamia Nuts, Almonds, Sesame Seeds (Tahini), Other Nuts and Seeds

Sources of Fat*			
Good	Polyunsaturated Fat	Omega-6	Plant Sources: Grape Seed Oil, Sunflower Oil, Corn Oil, Nuts, Seeds, Grains, Avocado Animal Sources: Eggs, Chicken, Dairy, Beef
		Omega-3	Plant Sources: Flaxseed Oil, Walnuts, Chia Seeds, Leafy Green Vegetables, Seaweed (Chlorella, Spirulina, etc.), Other Nuts and Seeds Animal Sources: Cold Water Fish, Egg Yolk
Good	Medium- and Short-Chain Saturated Fat	Plant Sources: Coconut and Palm Kernel Oil Animal Sources: Dairy Products	
Bad	Long-Chain Saturated Fat	Animal Fat (Pork, Beef, Lamb) and Dairy Products	
Bad	Trans Fat	Partially Hydrogenated Oils from Processed Foods	

*Most sources of fat contain multiple types of fat, but the foods listed in this table contain a majority of a specific type of fat. For example, safflower oil is 70 percent monounsaturated fat, while it does contain small amounts of other types of fat.

So how much fat should we eat? I generally recommend on the higher side, around half a gram per body weight. This is because I consider healthy fats to be extremely important for our body. They protect our brains, balance our hormonal systems, transport fat-soluble vitamins, and so on. Generally, a third of your caloric intake should be healthy fat. However, I do not recommend strict calorie counting simply because it, psychologically speaking, can create obsessive-compulsive behaviors, which is counterproductive to the life God wants for us.

Of your fat intake, there is no exact ratio for fat types; however, the majority of dietary fat should come from monounsaturated fats (plants) and a minority of polyunsaturated fats (plants, fish, and land animals). The polyunsaturated portion should ideally be split into a three-to-one ratio for omega-3s to -6s (fish fat to animal fat). This is the opposite of the typical American diet, in which there is about a ten-to-one ratio of omega-6s (red meat) to omega-3s (fish) and only about 30 percent monounsaturated fat.[33]

Here is a chart of proper fat intake:

Total Fat Intake Chart		
Your Body Weight = _____ x 0.5 = _____ Total Grams of Fat to Eat Everyday		
Approximate Fat Intake Distribution		
50% Mono- unsaturated Fat	50% Polyunsaturated Fat in a ratio of 3:1 Omega-3s to Omega 6s	
	3:1	
	37.5% Omega-3s	12.5% Omega-6s
Total Fat = ___ x 0.5 = _____ Grams	Total Fat ___ x 0.375 = _____ Grams	Total Fat ___ x 0.125 = _____ Grams

In addition to eating the proper types of fats and eating them in the right quantities, it is important to utilize cofactors in order to improve our overall fat metabolism. There are many vitamins and minerals that are either fat-soluble or assist in the metabolism of fat and the conversion of dietary fat into healthy fatty tissue in the body. If you are suffering from a major problem with your fat metabolism or have a disease involving the fat pathways, it is important to bolster or take more than enough of these cofactors until your body can normalize. Conversely, it is important to avoid the substances that hinder fat metabolism, especially if you are suffering from a fat metabolism imbalance. Here is a list of the most important fat metabolism cofactors and contradictions:

Fat Metabolism Cofactors	
Good	Magnesium, Zinc, Vitamin B, Vitamin C
Bad	Stress, Alcohol, Sugar, Steroids, Smoking

One last thing to note: good fat does have a shelf life, which means it will go rancid, or turn bad, under certain conditions. The first of these is time. Good fats have a substantially shorter life span than bad fats. (They lose their healthy properties even before humans can smell them going bad.) The second thing that destroys fat is oxygen. Especially with regard to oils, unsaturated oils are more likely to react to oxygen and degrade over time. This is accelerated by light and heat, so it is important to keep them in a cool, dark area. (This is also why olive oil comes in dark jars.)

Finally fat does have a "smoke point," a temperature at which they burn and lose their healthy properties. Therefore, it is important not to use low heat oils for high heat cooking or else you lose their intrinsic benefits. Here is a table of the smoke points for various healthy oils:

Fat Temperature Ratings		
Avocado Oil	520	Frying
Rice Bran Oil	490	
Palm Oil	450	
Sunflower Oil	450	
Peanut Oil	440	Baking or Sautéing
Hazelnut Oil	430	
Almond Oil	420	
Grapeseed Oil	420	
Sesame Oil	410	
Macadamia Nut Oil	390	
Coconut Oil	350	
Hemp Seed Oil	330	Dressings/Dips
Extra Virgin Olive Oil	320	

*Any of the higher smoke point oils can be used for lower temperature purposes, but lower temperature oils cannot be used for high temperature purposes without burning and losing their nutritional value.

CARBOHYDRATES

Carbohydrates are molecules primarily used for fuel for our bodies. Sometimes they serve other purposes, such as D-Ribose, which is used for making DNA. However, most carbohydrates are used for energy because they are the easiest and quickest molecules to break down. When they are broken down, they release energy. Specifically they release four calories per gram. Thus, carbohydrates are analogous to disposable batteries. This can be beneficial when they are used properly or extremely toxic if used improperly.

Carbohydrates are classified into three categories: simple, complex, and refined. Simple carbohydrates are the smallest and simplest molecules of sugar. Some examples of simple carbohydrates include glucose, fructose, and galactose. Simple carbohydrates usually taste sweet. This can be a blessing because it makes a lot of our foods have a naturally appealing taste, such as fruits, which are generally healthy and tasty when ingested in moderation.

Unfortunately we have taken simple carbohydrates and further refined them through synthetic processes in order to concentrate the sweetness. This produces a new synthetic type of sugar known as refined sugar, or refined carbohydrate. In this process, the sugars are softened, dissolved, and stripped of color. All additional components are removed, and the resulting powder is 99 percent sucrose. Refined sugars are then used abundantly in processed and prepared foods because of its extreme sweetness. This creates a serious health dilemma.

All refined sugars, especially sucrose, have been shown to cause a host of problems in the body. They are extremely toxic to the body. They promote heart disease, various types of cancers, diabetes, inflammatory diseases, and so many others. Their damage on our bodies are so widespread that not a system in the body can escape the damage. For example, refined sugars cause dental cavities in the teeth and increase musculoskeletal pain. They are even bad for the brain! The newest medical research labels Alzheimer's disease as "diabetes type III" because of the correlation between refined sugar damage to the brain and Alzheimer's.[34]

To make matters worse, most Americans consume dangerously excessive amounts of refined sugar every year. The average American eats about 150 pounds of sugar each year, and the average child will eat nearly their entire body weight in sugar each year. (This means that an average twelve-year-old will weigh about ninety pounds and will consume just under ninety pounds of sugar in a year's time span.)

As a result, the CDC predicts that one in three children born in the United States after the year 2000 will develop type 2 diabetes! This disease was previously unheard of in children because of its origin, which is completely due to lifestyle and diet.[35] These are all complications of refined sugars.

The Bible recommends that we do not adulterate our food supply, and if we do, we will be cursed with diseases. That is exactly what is happening with the epidemic of refined sugars. They are definitively contributing to disease, and we cannot produce health by masking those diseases with drug therapy. To enjoy the healthy life God designed for us, we must avoid refined sugars.

Fortunately, there is a type of carbohydrate that God designed for our bodies that is perfectly healthy for us, a complex carbohydrate. In complex carbohydrates, the simple sugars are strung together into very large and complex molecules, which makes them break down more slowly so they do not spike our blood sugar levels or damage our bodies when digested.

Complex carbohydrates are found naturally in vegetables, grains, lentils, some fruit, and so on. Basically the entire plant kingdom is comprised of complex carbs. These should constitute about half of all of our daily intake of calories. They have been shown to not only prevent but even to reduce some of the health problems caused by refined sugars. A meta study of sixty-four medical publications concluded that a diet high in complex carbohydrates, which come from fruits and vegetables, reduced the risk of coronary heart disease, cardiovascular disease, and total cancer and mortality from all causes, respiratory diseases, infectious diseases, diabetes, and all non-cardiovascular, non-cancer causes.[36] In addition, natural complex carbohydrate sources also contain a high density of nutrients for our bodies, such as vitamins, minerals, and phytonutrients, all of which we will discuss in depth later.

Unfortunately humans have adulterated our complex carbohydrate food sources as well. There are two specific processes we should be aware of: refinement and enrichment. With refined complex carbs, such as refined grain or refined rice, most all of the nutritional value has been stripped out of the food, and roughly 25 percent of the protein has been lost as well.[37] This allows it to have a longer shelf life and to be tastier. It also undergoes other chemical processes to make it more visually appealing, such as bleaching the color to white. These processes ruin the point of eating the food in the first place as it loses nearly all of its nutritional value and also develops some unhealthy properties. Refined complex carbs should be avoided at all costs.

The second synthetic process is known as enrichment, and while that sounds like a good term, it is not. In enrichment, they take complex carbs that have been fully refined (i.e., stripped of their nutritional value) and add back in five nutrients: iron, thiamin, riboflavin, niacin, and folic acid.

This seems noble, yet because the flour was refined to begin with, it still lacks all of its other nutrients that were stripped in the first place (e.g., magnesium, zinc, vitamins B6 and E, chromium, fiber, etc.). Enriched foods can also sometimes be labeled as "fortified" if the nutrients added were not in the original food. An example is milk fortified with vitamin D. Since vitamin D was not originally in the milk, it is labeled as "fortified." Yet the milk still went through the homogenizing process to kill or denature all healthy enzymes and proteins, and on the shelf, it is more or less a "dead" food. The bioavailability of these enriched nutrients is very low, which means that our bodies will not absorb very much of them because they are not natural.

Another major problem with our complex carbohydrate food supply is the genetic modification of its DNA. This is specifically forbidden in the Bible. "You shall not sow your field with two kinds of seed" (Leviticus 19:19 ESV). This sacrifices the nutritional value of the food in favor of some other attribute, such as longer shelf life, hardiness against certain bugs, or whatever. For example, in an article published by MomsAcrossAmerica and written by an employee of De Dell Seed Company, genetically modified corn contained 437 times less calcium, 56 times less magnesium, and 7 times less manganese than non-GMO corn.

This is going on in a mass scale with our food sources and has even been taken to a whole new level with lab DNA splicing. With lab DNA splicing, they take the DNA of other multiple organisms and splice them together. The dangers of genetically modifying organisms are truly frightening since we don't even know the extent of the damage that it could be causing long term. The US FDA generally considers genetically modified organisms, or GMOs, to be safe, but I highly recommend that they be avoided at all costs until long-term consequences can be ascertained and studied. Many other countries have outlawed them until they can be further studied.

An example of a GMO organism is a type of corn called BT corn. It was genetically created by splicing the DNA of a toxic soil bacteria into corn. In doing so, the corn would intrinsically create a toxin that killed the stomach lining of whatever ate it. This killed off most of the insects that traditionally kill corn crops but could be damaging to humans as well. Several studies demonstrate that it is damaging to other mammals on the planet,[38] and one study published in the *Journal of Applied Toxicology* showed that it was damaging to humans.[39]

More alarming is the fact that BT corn (and other GMO foods) exist in our bodies, meaning we have been readily eating them. The *Journal of Reproductive Toxicology* published a study showing BT corn toxins to exist in the bloodstreams of 93 percent of pregnant women, 80 percent of unborn children, and 69 percent of non-pregnant women tested. This study also showed other GMOs in their bloodstreams as well.[40]

Sadly, most of the packaged complex carbs in the grocery stores are either refined, enriched, fortified, GMO, or synthetically altered in some other way. Furthermore, if it is boxed or packaged, it is loaded with preservatives because natural food does not have a long shelf life.

This is not the food that God designed for us to eat, and it does not create healthiness in the body. Eating these things will slowly starve our bodies of the nutrients they need and push us toward chronic disease. The best types of carbohydrates are the natural forms of carbohydrates with minimal processing. They should be consumed in a one-to-two ratio (simple to complex) and should make up at least 50 percent of our caloric intake. This means that half of everything we eat should be fruits, vegetables, beans, legumes, nuts, and seeds. Of those categories, we should have two servings of vegetables (or beans, legumes, nuts, or seeds) for every serving of fruit. This will stimulate tremendous healing in our bodies by providing the perfect ratio of complex to simple carbohydrates while not burdening our metabolic systems with artificial carbohydrates. This also loads our bodies with vitamins, minerals, and other nutrients since these foods have the highest density of those healing molecules of any type of food on the planet per calorie. By God's design, they would synergize perfectly with our bodies to promote the healthiest lifestyle possible. They would constantly infuse our bodies with energy while also providing everything they need to heal, repair, and function in the best possible way.

PHYTONUTRIENTS

Besides not eating the right type of carbohydrates or eating enough of the good carbohydrates, the average American also does not eat enough variety of the good carbohydrates. Statistically speaking, the average person in American gets the majority of all of their vegetable intake from only two sources: potatoes and tomatoes, in the form of French fries and ketchup (or pizza sauce).[41] This poses a serious problem for our health since God created nearly a million species of plants that can be used for the health of our bodies. Within this variety, there is an assortment of nutrients, phytonutrients, that are spread out among the various species of plants. Furthermore, these phytonutrients are only found in the plant kingdom and cannot be found in any other food source. Phytonutrients are extremely beneficial for us. Many of them have tremendous healing effects on the body and can be used broadly for general health or concentrated for a medicinal effect.

Actually that medicinal philosophy is the foundation on which our current health-care system was built. Before mankind had synthetic drugs, people ate plants and herbs all the time to heal themselves of ailments. An even better way to utilize the phytonutrients is to incorporate them generously into our daily diet plans before we ever develop sickness so they can constantly prevent our bodies from falling into disease processes. The Greek physician Hippocrates once said, "Let food be thy medicine and medicine be thy food." If we eat the food God designed for us, in the correct variety, these phytonutrients will heal us before we ever get sick and literally make our bodies resilient.

Phytonutrients can be categorized by the pigment, or color, of the foods they are found in. Literally, plant foods with different colors will contain different phytonutrients. This is not to be confused with synthetic color additives that are found in packaged foods and are extremely harmful for our bodies. But with phytonutrients, each color found in the plant kingdom represents different healing attributes, and they can be mixed and matched synergistically for our health benefit.

For example, lycopene can be found in red foods such as tomatoes and watermelons. Lycopene is a molecule related to vitamin A, but with different healing properties. It is a powerful protector of the heart and prostate glands and is also a great antioxidant and anticancer molecule. It is recommended that our diets include lycopene.

Beta-carotene can be found in orange fruits and vegetables such as carrots, yams, and sweet potatoes. It is a precursor for vitamin A but is more potent than synthetically created vitamin A. Beta-carotene functions as a strong antioxidant and is especially healthy for the eyes, skin, mucous glands, digestive system, and bones.

The yellow-orange pigments found in citrus fruits are vitamin C and flavonoids. These are some of the most potent antioxidants. Vitamin C and flavonoids affect nearly everything in the body, including boosting the immune system, repairing soft tissue, and even improving bone strength.[42] Oranges, lemons, grapefruits, papayas, and peaches all contain these phytonutrients. Be wary of grapefruits though if you are taking a lot of prescription drugs, as they cross-react with some pharmaceutical drugs and cancel out their effects.

The green pigment found in leafy greens is known as folate, or vitamin B9. The term "folate" actually comes from the same Latin word as "foliage," which means "leaves." Folate is extremely important for our health. Low folate levels are associated with increased cancer risk, cardiovascular disease, cognitive diminishment, anemia, congenital anomalies in babies, and much, much more. It affects so much because it is utilized at a cellular level for healthy DNA replication and repair. It also neutralizes homocysteine, a major inflammatory molecule in our bodies and an independent risk factor for cardiovascular disease and stroke.

The green-white pigment in vegetables such as broccoli, Brussels sprouts, cauliflower, cabbage, and so forth are known as indoles and lutein. These are potent detoxifiers, which means they remove unwanted toxins from the body by enhancing "phase I detoxification" in the body, which is where the body makes a toxin more water-soluble so it is less reactive and can be excreted through our waste. Indoles also contribute to hormonal balance by eliminating excessive estrogen in the body. They also fight cancer in two ways: inducing apoptosis within the cancer cells (basically programmed cell death) and inhibiting angiogenesis (preventing the cancer cell from reproducing).

The white-green vegetables such as garlic, onions, chives, and asparagus contain aliyl sulfides, very powerful immune system modulators and detoxification stimulators. They have demonstrated amazing anticancer properties for several types of cancers.[43] They also protect against age-related neurodegeneration[44] and are healthy for the cardiovascular system and many other systems in the body.

The blue color in foods are anthocyanins, which have a broad range of health and maintenance effects on the body. In fact, scientists have not even scratched the surface of all of the health benefits of anthocyanins. Anthocyanins have been observed to protect cellular DNA from degradation, assist in regulating the immune system, and protect against bad fat metabolism. They even strengthen blood vessels and reduce blood pressure. Anthocyanins are some of the most important phytonutrients we can take, and I recommend that you try to get some into your daily diet.

Resveratrol causes the purple found in grapes, plums, berries, and other plants. Resveratrol protects against inflammation and age-related diseases. Resveratrol has been shown to inhibit the spread of cancer, specifically prostate cancer, throughout the body, which is something that cancer likes to do. Resveratrol has also demonstrated preventative qualities with regard to brain diseases such as Alzheimer's. In a lot of ways, it has been known to minimize the effects of aging and is one of the most important phytonutrients available to us.

These phytonutrients make food vibrant, fun, and appealing to arrange. They showcase God's great creative talent and His engineering genius. As an aside, I believe this balance between creativity and logic is an attribute that humans were created to emulate. Most people lack this balance, overdeveloping either one side of the brain or the other. Right-brained people become overtly artistic while left-brained people are overtly logical. This can become a fault if a person becomes too unbalanced. Fortunately science demonstrates that our brains have the capability of changing. According to science, our brains have plasticity, the ability to rewire themselves based on stimuli. In other words, if we are extremely logical, we can and should spend time developing our artistic side and vice versa.

Thousands of years before all of this, the Bible said to be "transformed by the renewing of your mind" (Romans 12:2 NIV). In other words, we should emulate God's great intrinsic balance within our own brains to be both creative and logical. The Bible says, "The heavens declare the glory of God," and I believe that phytonutrients are simply another example of that. They are beautifully colorful and engineered on a molecular level to be profoundly healing to our bodies.

In addition, I consider the color palette of phytonutrients to be a unique parallel to the blessing God made with Noah and mankind after the flood in Genesis 9, "This is the sign of the covenant I am making between me and you and every living creature with you, a covenant for all generations to come: I have set my rainbow in the clouds, and it will be the sign of the covenant between me and the earth."

God created and arranged the colors of the rainbow as a sign of a blessing for us. And with food, God created the rainbow of phytonutrients and promised health to all people who observed it. "You shall serve the LORD your God, and He will bless your bread and your water, and will take sickness away from among you" (Exodus 23:25 ESV).

I hope you are beginning to see that God's laws in the Bible are an explanation of natural law, and within that law, there is a great wealth of information about life and health. He was not trying to restrict our diets; He was trying to expand them. Therefore, if we want to live the healthy life that He designed for us, we should begin to incorporate more phytonutrients into our diets.

As a rule of thumb, I generally recommend that everyone eats at least one food from each of the color groups each day so their plates are as colorful as possible. Here is a quick chart to use as a brief overview of some of the more pronounced phytonutrients and their benefits:

Phytonutrients: God's Natural Food Coloring			
Red	Lycopene	Tomatoes, Watermelon, Guava	Antioxidant, Anticancer, Cardiovascular Health, Stroke Risk Reduction
Orange	Beta-Carotene	Carrots, Yams, Sweet Potatoes, Mangos, Pumpkin	Antioxidant, Skin and Eye Health
Yellow	Vitamin C, Flavonoids	Oranges, Lemons, Papaya, Peaches, Grapefruit	Immune Booster, Cancer Growth Inhibitor, Detoxifier

Phytonutrients: God's Natural Food Coloring			
Green	Folate	Spinach, Kale, Collard Greens	Healthy Cellular Metabolism, DNA Repair, Brain Function
Green/ White	Indoles	Broccoli, Brussels Sprouts, Bok Choy, Cabbage, Cauliflower, Collard Greens, Kale	Detoxification Upregulator, Carcinogen Eliminator, Hormonal Stability
White/ Green	Allyl Sulfides	Garlic, Onion, Chives, Leeks, Asparagus	Detoxification Upregulator, Cancer Cell Destroyer, Immune System Booster
Blue	Anthocyanins	Blueberries, Blackberries, Cherries, Grapes, Plums, Prunes	Antioxidant, Anti-inflammatory, Anticancer, Antiviral
Purple	Resveratrol	Grapes, Berries, Cocoa, Pistachios	Antioxidant, Cardiovascular Health, Inflammation Reducer, Cancer Suppressor

VITAMINS

Beyond the three major macronutrients, there are also micronutrients that are vital to our long-term health, vitamins and minerals. This chapter will provide a brief overview of vitamins followed by a more specific discussion of each individual one.

God designed vitamins to perform many chemical reactions in the body. They often function like pseudo-hormones because they control and regulate so many biological processes. They are absolutely necessary for good health. A deficiency in any vitamin will lead to illness or disease. The human body requires thirteen vitamins for proper health: vitamin A (retinol), vitamin B1 (thiamine), vitamin B2 (riboflavin), vitamin B3 (niacin), vitamin B5 (pantothenic acid), vitamin B6 (pyridoxine), vitamin B7 (biotin), vitamin B9 (folate), vitamin B12 (cobalamin), vitamin C (ascorbic acid), vitamin D (cholecalciferol), vitamin E (tocopherol), and vitamin K (quinone).

When tested, about 70 percent of the US adult population consumed lower than optimal amounts of vitamins, and 10 percent were completely deficient in at least one micronutrient.[45] This is a serious problem associated with processed food diets. The average American diet lacks natural, unprocessed, biblical foods, which have the highest density of vitamins and minerals. Let me state that again: fruits and vegetables have the highest density of vitamins and minerals per calorie of all food sources.

Supplementing vitamins is extremely safe. According to the American Association of Poison Control Centers, "In 2004, the deaths of 3 people [in the US] were attributed to the intake of vitamins,"[46] and the medical journal *Toxicology* states, "In 2010, not one single person [in the US] died as a result of taking vitamins."[47]

Just compare this to the number of people who died as a result of an adverse reaction or a cross-reaction with properly prescribed, properly administered pharmaceutical drugs—128,000 deaths per year, with an additional 1.9 million hospitalizations per year. (This does not include misprescribing, overdosing, or self-prescribing, which would bring this number to 2.74 million/year.)[48]

I recommend shifting toward a more natural, biblical diet to bolster the intake of naturally occurring vitamins. I also suggest supplementing a good multivitamin to cover any deficiencies that could occur in the diet. In the following chapters, we will discuss each family of vitamins: their purposes, effects, and associated signs of deficiencies.

VITAMIN A

The vitamins are labeled by letters according to the order in which they were discovered. The first one to be discovered was vitamin A, an antioxidant necessary for healthy skin and eyes. Vitamin A is found in the highest concentrations in chili peppers, carrots, sweet potatoes, mangos, collard greens, and spinach. The daily recommended amount is 2,500–5,000 international units (IUs) a day. If you are in acute deficiency (below the minimal amount in a pathological way), then the therapeutic dosage is 50,000 IUs per day for one to two days. A deficiency in vitamin A will cause keratinization, or hardening of the skin, most commonly on the backs of the arms or legs, but they can occur in any skinlike tissue, even in the stomach lining.

Vitamin A deficiencies are rare in the United States, but most people do not get a maximum dose either. Therefore, I recommend always making sure that you eat foods containing vitamin A.

VITAMIN B1

The next vitamins discovered were a group of vitamins labeled as "B vitamins." Though they share the same label, they are actually all very chemically different. Vitamin B1, or thiamin, potentiates and mimics acetylcholine, which is important for energy production, DNA replication, and mental clarity. It is found in whole grains, brown rice, sunflower seeds, peanuts, and so forth. It requires magnesium to be activated, which is why it is important to get B1 from natural sources where it is coupled with magnesium. Synthetic B1 isn't always bioavailable to the body. Alcohol inhibits vitamin B1, which is why people seem to get moody when they have been drinking.

Deficiencies in B1 cause mental fog, muscle pains, and irregular heartbeats. The symptoms can get severe if the deficiency is severe enough and can cause permanent brain damage or death, although these cases are rare in Western civilization.

VITAMIN B2

The next vitamin is vitamin B2, or riboflavin. It is found in nuts and seeds (especially almonds), whole grains, and some mushrooms. Vitamin B2 is useful for energy production. It also regenerates glutathione, a potent antioxidant. It also increases total iron-binding capacity of the blood. For these reasons, it has been used in the past to naturally treat and/or prevent many common ailments, for example, anemia, migraines, and cataracts. Studies demonstrate that vitamin B2 reduces the incidence of esophageal cancer by 14 percent.[49]

A deficiency in B2 usually presents as cracked lips in the corners of the mouth (angular cheilitis). The normal dosage of vitamin B2 is 5–10 milligrams per day. For migraine prevention, nutritionists recommend 400 milligrams. As a side note, antimalarial drugs interfere with B2. So if you are traveling and need to take antimalarial drugs, you might consider loading up on B2 before and after the trip.

VITAMIN B3

Vitamin B3, or niacin, has variations known as "nicotinic acid" or "niacinamide." It is found in eggs, fish, whole grains, peanuts, chili peppers, and legumes. Nicotinic acid has been shown in studies to lower blood pressure[50] and bad cholesterol.[51] However, it can also cause flushed skin and liver damage in extremely high doses over long periods of time. (So it should not be the main way in which you control cholesterol.)

Inositol hexaniacinate, the safest form of vitamin B3, has been shown to improve Raynaud's (cold/numb fingers and toes) and intermittent claudication (cramping of muscles after exercise due to blood vessel constriction). Inositol hexaniacinate also improves insulin sensitivity (as it helps regulate blood sugar levels) and lowers blood fat. Niacinamide has been shown clinically, but not through research, to help manage the pain from rheumatoid arthritis. Vitamin B3 also improves DNA repair and thus has been shown to reduce precancerous skin lesions and skin cancer relapses.[52] The safest form of B3 is inositol hexaniacinate.

VITAMIN B5

Vitamin B5 is known as pantothenic acid. Pantothenic acid deficiency is rare. However, the vitamin can still be useful in some situations. It is often used as an anti-stress, adrenal support supplement when bundled with vitamin C. It also enhances the effectiveness of carnitine and CoQ10, so it can be bundled with those supplements for a greater effect as well.

VITAMIN B6

Vitamin B6, or pyridoxine, is important for cell replication, neurotransmitter synthesis, and much more. It is best found in whole grains, nuts, legumes, bananas, avocados, kale, and spinach. Pyridoxine has been shown to decrease the severity of asthma due to tryptophan and serotonin production improvements. It can be combined with cobalamin (B12) and folic acid (B9) to reduce systemic homocysteine levels.

Homocysteine is an inflammatory marker in the body that is associated with heart attacks, strokes, Alzheimer's, dementia, and other acute inflammatory diseases. Therefore, these vitamins can help lower cholesterol and blood pressure as well as the risk of these disease processes associated with homocysteine.

Pyridoxine is also a mild diuretic. It also helps with diabetic neuropathies (tingling or numbness in hands and feet due to diabetes). Combined with vitamin E, magnesium, and black cohosh, pyridoxine improves premenstrual syndrome. Food coloring, oral contraceptives, alcohol, and excessive protein are all antagonists to pyridoxine (B6). Therefore, if you are consuming any of those, you should be attentive to also consume foods that contain pyridoxine (B6).

Sources of pyridoxine include beef, poultry, starchy vegetables, and non-citrus fruits. In addition, it requires the other B vitamins, specifically riboflavin, along with magnesium to be converted to an active form in the body. Therefore, natural food sources of B6 are the best sources, as opposed to synthetic formulations or fortifications.

VITAMIN B7

Vitamin B7, or biotin, is necessary for strong hair, skin, and nails. If you are suffering from thin or brittle hair and nails, you are probably deficient in biotin. It synergizes well with the other B vitamins and CoQ10. Alcohol consumption and poor gastrointestinal bacteria inhibits it; therefore, its bioavailability increases when consumed in a natural way, from minimally processed, natural foods. The best sources of biotin include soybeans, brown rice, peanuts, walnuts, barley, oats, and legumes.

VITAMIN B9

Vitamin B9 is known as folate. The synthetic version of it is folic acid or folinic acid. Folate deficiency is extremely common. In fact, it is the most common vitamin deficiency in the world. Even Americans who get an adequate amount of folate usually are on the lower end of normal. Symptoms of folate deficiency include mental fatigue, forgetfulness, irritability, inflammation in the mouth (swollen tongue or gingivitis), inflammation in the intestines (diarrhea, irritable bowel mimicry, and loss of appetite), and even shortness of breath or heart palpitations. Low folate levels can also impair brain function to the point of functional depression. (In these cases, the person will not respond to antidepressants because what they really need is a functional dose of folate.) Folate deficiencies in pregnant mothers can produce birth defects in their children. Therefore, it is especially important for expecting mothers to supplement with folate.

Folate comes from the Latin word *Foli*, which means "leaf" or "foliage." Folate, therefore, is found primarily in green leafy vegetables and other dark green vegetables such as asparagus and Brussels sprouts. It can also be found, to a lesser degree, in fruits, nuts, seeds, peas, and whole grains. The normal RDA values for daily consumption of folate is 400 micrograms for adults and 600 micrograms for pregnant women.

However, since it is the most common vitamin deficiency, I generally recommend consuming more than the minimum requirement. It is water-soluble so it is not harmful to consume too much, and any excess folate in your system will just be dissolved and excreted in your urine.

VITAMIN B12

The last B vitamin is B12, or cobalamin. The most common form of B12 is cyanocobalamin, and the most active form is methylcobalamin. B12 is the largest vitamin by molecular weight, and it is only produced by bacteria but is found in animal meat because they have bacteria in their guts. Therefore, it is very easy to become deficient in B12, especially if you are fully vegetarian or have lost gastrointestinal integrity due to aging or poor diet.

Cobalamin is extremely important for the brain, nervous system, blood cells, and DNA replication. Therefore, a deficiency of cobalamin can manifest as problems in those areas. Even minor deficiencies will induce fatigue, depression, moodiness, memory loss, headaches, and so on. And more moderate to extreme deficiencies can cause anemia (not enough red blood cells) as well as serious brain and nervous system damage. Excess vitamin B12 without supplementation is a sign of a possible significant underlying health problem and should be investigated with a full diagnostic work-up in order to determine the possibility of disease.

VITAMIN C

Vitamin C is one of the most important vitamins. It is used throughout the body as an antioxidant or anti-aging molecule for the cells. It is also an important cofactor for creating new healthy cells. It also increases the potency of other types of antioxidant healing molecules, such as bioflavonoids and vitamin E. It is good for the brain, heart, skin, tendons, and pretty much every other system in the body. It also improves fertility for both men[53] and women,[54] and it can help reduce excess bleeding from menstrual irregularities because it helps bind iron in the blood. It decreases pain in the body. It is good for histamine-related pathologies, such as asthma and allergies. It builds healthy blood and blood vessels. In one study, vitamin C reduced the risk of having a stroke by almost 50 percent.[55] Vitamin C is also conveniently toxic to cancer cells.[56] As healing as it is to normal cells, it is equally destructive to unhealthy cells. And with regard to cancer treatments, it has been shown to double the effectiveness of chemotherapy and radiation therapy.[57]

Importantly, vitamin C does not harm the body, even in large quantities. You can take it up to bowel tolerance, and it will never have a toxic effect on the body. Bowel tolerance means that as your body needs more, you will digest more and leave the rest behind. Therapeutically, you can increase dosage until you get diarrhea and then back down until your gut normalizes, which would be the functional limit that your body can absorb. It is functionally nontoxic because your body will never absorb more than it can handle.

Linus Pauling, who was a founder of molecular biology and quantum chemistry and is the only person to ever win two unshared Nobel prizes, used vitamin C in extremely high doses intravenously to heal all kinds of diseases in the body before the medical community began to widely discredit his work on vitamin C and health due to his lack of a medical degree.

Deficiency in vitamin C causes scurvy, a major bleeding disorder. While full-blown scurvy is not often seen these days, many people suffer from mild forms of vitamin C deficiency, including weak gums and teeth, lethargy, easy bleeding/bruising, nosebleeds, slow wound repair, and clumping or corkscrewing of hair. Fortunately, improving levels of vitamin C in the body can almost immediately reverse these symptoms. The best sources of vitamin C include acerola cherries, citrus fruits, and leafy green vegetables.

VITAMIN D

Vitamin D is one of the most important vitamins. In fact, it functions as more of a hormone than a vitamin, helping synthesize neurotransmitters in the brain, modulating the long-term immune system, and increasing calcium absorption. Unfortunately, the majority of all Americans are deficient in vitamin D. Vitamin D is created in the deep layers of our skin when we are exposed to natural sunlight. It is specifically produced from UVB rays. This means vitamin D production is blocked by windows, indirect light, and sunscreen. UVB is also a shorter wavelength, so the light exposure must be when the sun is greater than 45 degrees above the horizon.

Therefore, for optimal vitamin D production, it is recommended that you get direct sunlight between the hours of 10:00 a.m. and 2:00 p.m. for fifteen to thirty minutes, several times a week. If you are deficient in vitamin D, you can improve your vitamin D production by reactivating vitamin D receptors by using resveratrol supplementation.[58] You can also increase the amount of days that you are receiving direct sunlight, although I don't recommend extending the amount of time you are in the sun. You can also increase the surface area of the body exposed to the sun. The best places for absorption are the torso—stomach and back.

In addition, you need several cofactors to produce vitamin D: magnesium, zinc, boron, vitamin A, and vitamin K. It is recommended that, at a minimum, you get at least 200 to 400 units a day of vitamin D. However, 4,000 IUs of vitamin D daily have been shown to greatly enhance a person's biochemical processes and their sense of well-being.[59] In addition, if your body is in need, it can actually produce and use up to 10,000 IUs a day, which is great news for anyone recovering from a chronic illness or disease process.

VITAMIN E

Vitamin E is also known as tocopherol, which means "to bear offspring." It was named as such because it has historically been used to improve fertility. In reality, it doesn't improve fertility beyond a certain threshold, but it does drive pathways that can cause infertility if you are deficient in vitamin E. It is a fat-soluble vitamin, so it must be consumed with fat, and it is found naturally in healthy fat foods: almonds, seeds, plant oils, dark leafy greens, and avocados. A powerful fat antioxidant, it is vital to the brain, nervous system, and steroid hormone development. (Steroid hormones are derived from healthy fat.)

It also acts as a natural blood thinner because healthy fats displace unhealthy gunky fats in the blood stream. Be wary of artificial, petroleum-derived vitamin E (dl-alpha-tocopherol) because it has been shown to increase cancer, whereas naturally occurring vitamin E (d-alpha-tocopherol) has been shown to reduce cancer.[60]

The recommended minimum RDA values for vitamin E are around 22 IUs a day, but I generally recommend upwards of 400 IUs a day, not exceeding 1,000 a day, all from natural sources.

VITAMIN K

Vitamin K is an extremely important vitamin that is a significant cofactor for binding calcium. Therefore, it is useful in bone, cardiovascular, metabolic, and even brain health. Studies have shown that it can help prevent Alzheimer's disease[61] and diabetes, and it can also reduce bruising[62] and improve blood coagulation (clotting). Also, having inadequate amounts of vitamin K can dramatically increase your risk of both heart disease and stroke by allowing calcium to be deposited into your blood vessels, thus hardening them and preventing proper blood flow.

Vitamin K can be further subdivided into K1 and K2. K1, or phylloquinone, is found in dark green leafy vegetables. It is not as easily absorbed as K2, but it can be converted into K2 in our intestines by our gut bacteria. Therefore, it is very important to supplement with probiotics and/or fermented foods if you have ever taken antibiotics because antibiotics can decrease your vitamin K2 production by over 70 percent by wiping out your good gut bacteria.[63]

Vitamin K1 is found in the highest concentrations in cooked kale, spinach, collard greens, turnip greens, broccoli, Brussels sprouts, cabbage, and asparagus. This is one instance where cooking your food yields a higher concentration of a nutrient than eating it raw. Vitamin K1 is fat-soluble, so it must be cooked and consumed with a healthy fat in order for the body to properly absorb it.

Vitamin K2, or menaquinone, is found in fermented foods or converted from K1 in the intestines. It is found in the highest concentrations in natto (fermented soy). Another good source is brie and Gouda cheeses. It can also be found in grass-fed poultry such as chicken and turkey as well as butter. It is recommended that you eat between 200 and 280 micrograms of vitamin K per day.

CHOLINE

Choline is a vitamin-like essential nutrient. We need choline for certain neurotransmitter syntheses. We can produce a small amount of choline in our liver, but most people do not produce adequate amounts without a biblical diet because most of the choline precursors are in fish, eggs, nuts, seeds, and legumes. Choline is beneficial for the brain, liver, and muscles. It has been shown to enhance our memory and even improve the long-term memory of children born to mothers who supplemented choline while they were in utero.[64] The most bioavailable form of choline is phosphatidylcholine, and a cheaper version is known as lecithin. It is important to make sure to include fish, eggs, nuts, seeds, and legumes in your biblical diet.

INOSITOL

Inositol, another vitamin-like chemical that is very good for our bodies, was once considered to be vitamin B8, but it was discovered that our bodies can make it in smaller quantities so we don't necessarily need to get it from our foods. However, most Americans have low levels of inositol. Fortunately, the designer's diet includes plenty of inositol-rich foods: citrus fruits, whole grains, nuts, seeds, and legumes.

Inositol is involved in multiple pathways in the body such as balancing blood sugar and hormones. It is also a very potent mood enhancer and neurotransmitter stabilizer, like the other B vitamins. Therefore, inositol has been traditionally used for depression, anxiety, obsessive-compulsive disorder, insomnia, and nerve pain and has even shown evidence of improving symptoms associated with Alzheimer's.

On the hormonal side, it has been used for polycystic ovarian syndrome and testosterone dysregulation and for diminishing mood swings associated with PMS and PMDD. Along with biotin, inositol encourages healthy hair growth. The plant form of inositol, or phytic acid, contains very powerful anticancer properties.

MINERALS

Minerals are inorganic compounds that are found naturally all over the earth. We get them when we eat plant foods that are grown in mineral-rich soil or from animals who have eaten plants from mineral-rich soil. This can be a problem in the United States because we do not follow God's design for soil management and have depleted our soil of many of the essential minerals. For example, the human body contains over sixty minerals, with sixteen being essential for proper growth, but most farmers only fertilize with nitrogen and phosphorus because those two are the only minerals necessary for growing larger plants and most crops are sold by weight or quantity.

In addition, most farmers do not rotate their crops, or rest their land, which results in a depletion of the mineral count. In the Bible, God commanded that every seventh year there were to be no crops planted in fields (to let the nutrients replenish) (Exodus 23:10; Leviticus 25:4).

In addition, in that seventh year, the people were to allow wild animals to infiltrate the land, feed off the land, and establish natural ecosystems with the land, thus restoring more of the land's natural resources such as minerals and water. God designed this system to create long-term, sustainable, nutrient-rich soil for the crops for the next cycle of six years. It also created rhythm to life.

> For everything there is a season, and a time for every
> matter under heaven: a time to be born, and a time to die;
> a time to plant, and a time to pluck up what is planted; a
> time to kill, and a time to heal; a time to break down, and
> a time to build up; a time to weep, and a time to laugh; a
> time to mourn, and a time to dance; a time to cast away

stones, and a time to gather stones together; a time to embrace, and a time to refrain from embracing; a time to seek, and a time to lose; a time to keep, and a time to cast away; a time to tear, and a time to sew; a time to keep silence, and a time to speak; a time to love, and a time to hate; a time for war, and a time for peace. (Ecclesiastes 3:1–13)

What gain has the worker from his toil? I have seen the business that God has given to the children of man to be busy with. He has made everything beautiful in its time. Also, he has put eternity into man's heart, yet so that he cannot find out what God has done from the beginning to the end. I perceived that there is nothing better for them than to be joyful and to do good as long as they live; also that everyone should eat and drink and take pleasure in all his toil—this is God's gift to man. (Ecclesiastes 3:1–13 ESV)

That rhythm of life was actually given to us as a gift from God (verse 13) in order to break the cycle of monotony and to rejuvenate the ecosystem. As our society has abandoned these simple principles, we pay the price by overworking our bodies and overtaxing our land. I would encourage everyone to practice crop rotation in their farms and gardens along with soil rejuvenation practices such as composting.

With regards to your diet, I strongly recommend supplementation with minerals every day to alleviate what has been lost in the soil and food. Since minerals are inorganic (i.e., not created synthetically but harvested from the earth), they are safe to supplement.

There are sixteen essential minerals and over sixty trace minerals (since they are only used in small amounts), and each plays a uniquely important role in the healthiness of our bodies. Many minerals are so influential that they can dramatically affect our lives without us even realizing it. For example, low magnesium or potassium can cause muscle cramping. Since the heart is a muscle, severe deficiencies can cause heart arrhythmias or mistimed beats (preventricular contractions), which can be extremely dangerous and even cause fatality.

This is only one example out of millions of processes in our bodies.

Needless to say, minerals are vitally important to our health. God designed our bodies to utilize them, and as such, we must have the types of God-designed diets that include plenty of trace minerals.

Minerals also work hand in hand with vitamins for optimal performance in the body. Without minerals, vitamins would be less effective and vice versa. For example, iron is necessary to bind oxygen to our blood in order to be delivered to the cells of the body. One of the major cofactors, or helpers, in that reaction is vitamin C. Therefore, we need proper vitamin C to bind oxygen to iron in the blood. In order to acquire the kind of health that God designed us to have, we must have both vitamins and minerals in our bodies, in the appropriate amounts. In this chapter, we will discuss all sixteen essential minerals in detail and also list the trace minerals so you can be made aware of them.

IRON

Iron is one of the most important essential minerals. Unfortunately it is also the most commonly deficient mineral in the world and the United States. In fact, it is one of the few minerals that is predominantly lacking in both Third and First World countries. Approximately 30 percent of the entire world's population is deficient in iron.[65]

Iron deficiency is even mentioned in the Bible in Luke 8: 22 when Jesus, the Master Physician, brought a girl back to life and then immediately commanded that she be given meat to eat. (The literal Greek translation says "meat," even though most translations just say "food.") This indicates that she probably had died of severe anemia caused by a lack of iron.

The body uses iron in three main areas: the blood, the immune system, and brain function. A deficiency in iron can cause anemia, excessive menstrual bleeding, impaired immune function, fatigue, and brain fog. One of the earliest signs of low iron is restless leg syndrome, where you lay in bed at night squirming around because you cannot get comfortable.

The best sources of iron are kelp, blackstrap molasses, lentils, spinach, red meat, nuts and seeds, prunes, and raisins. The iron found in plants is called "non-heme" because it is not bound to blood proteins, whereas half of the iron found in animal sources is "heme," or bound to blood proteins. Our bodies more easily absorb heme iron.

However, non-heme iron is healthier for us because it does not cause an absorption of another animal's blood proteins into our system. In fact, too much heme iron can be difficult for our bodies to metabolize and is implicated in many disorders such as coronary heart disease (increase risk by 57 percent),[66] colon cancer,[67] and hemochromatosis. It is also being studied as being a possible cause of multiple sclerosis (MS) because MS sufferers demonstrate aberrant iron deposition in the brain on MRI brain scans.[68]

Non-heme iron appears to be healthier because it can be regulated, used, or removed by the body more easily. However, non-heme iron has a lower absorption rate than heme iron. Fortunately, non-heme iron is often bundled in nature with vitamin C, which dramatically improves its absorption. An example of non-heme iron source would be lentils, beans, and spinach. The recommended daily value for iron is between 15 and 20 milligrams per day. If you are deficient in iron, up to 30 milligrams a day may be taken in between meals as a supplement. (Don't forget to take with vitamin C for better absorption.) The best forms to supplement are ferrous fumarate or ferrous succinate. It also helps to cook with iron cookware, as small amounts of iron will leach into the food.

MAGNESIUM

Magnesium, one of the most commonly deficient and most important minerals in the body, is required for a lot of detoxification pathways such as glutathione production and toxin removal. It is also used for enzyme activation in energy production and for DNA replication inside cells. It also is important for muscle contraction, even within the heart and blood vessels. Overall, there are more than three hundred other chemical reactions in the body that utilize magnesium.[69] Therefore, a deficiency in magnesium can cause muscle cramps, heart arrhythmias, mental confusion, depression, fatigue, insomnia, and a whole host of other symptoms.

Unfortunately it is estimated that 80 percent of Americans do not get sufficient amounts of magnesium.[70] Some of the earliest signs of low magnesium include loss of appetite, headaches, fatigue, weakness, and insomnia. Another way to describe the feeling is "tired but wired." You feel anxious but don't have the energy to go do anything. It is important to normalize magnesium ingestion to restore balance to the body. The recommended daily intake for magnesium is 6 milligrams for every 2.2 pounds, which is between 300 and 400 milligrams per day, depending upon your body weight. Here is a table for easy conversion specific to your ody:

Your Weight = __ ÷ 2.2 x 6 __ Milligrams of Total Magnesium Needed

The best food sources of magnesium are green leafy vegetables, legumes, nuts, seeds, and whole grains. The most absorbable forms of magnesium in a supplement are magnesium citrate, magnesium malate, magnesium succinate, and magnesium fumarate. Magnesium shares its absorption channels with calcium, so high calcium or dairy diets can reduce magnesium absorption and vice versa. Interestingly, both minerals work together in the body as a team, so it is important that our ratio of magnesium to calcium remains healthy and balanced.

Fortunately, God's diet includes calcium and magnesium in perfect ratios. As long as we are eating plenty of natural, plant-based food groups and avoiding synthetic food chemicals, we should have no problem improving our magnesium intake and balancing our magnesium/calcium ratios.

CALCIUM

Calcium, another important essential mineral, is quite abundant in the body. The fifth-most abundant element in our bodies, it is absolutely vital to bone growth, nervous system function, blood clotting, tooth integrity, and even digestive system health. A deficiency in calcium can be catastrophic for our health. While calcium deficiencies are not as common as iron or magnesium, the majority of Americans still do not consume adequate amounts of calcium daily.[71] This could be caused by a deficiency in the soil and also from foods that inhibit calcium absorption. The biggest culprits are caffeine, alcohol, and phosphates (soft drinks). In addition, it is difficult to observe calcium deficiencies because it does not cause symptoms until it becomes a chronic condition such as rickets or osteoporosis.

The recommended daily intake of calcium is 1,000 to 1,200 milligrams for adults. Unfortunately, if you are low in calcium, you cannot megadose it because more than 2,000 milligrams a day can increase your risk of cardiovascular disease and kidney stones. In addition, excessive calcium inhibits magnesium digestion, which could lead to other problems. This balance would have been problematic for humans except that God designed our bodies to self-regulate calcium perfectly to protect us from extreme imbalances.

Scientific studies have shown that when we overload with calcium, our intestines become less efficient at absorbing it and our kidneys dump it out from our bodies faster. This process is reversed if we are restricted from calcium in our diet. Therefore, the best way to raise calcium levels in the body is to ingest bioavailable calcium from God's diet on a regular, daily basis until your levels normalize. The best sources of bioavailable calcium are green leafy vegetables (what cows eat in order to produce their milk), such as spinach and kale. These vegetables have the perfect balance of calcium and magnesium as well as the perfect pH to absorb them.

While the Bible prescribes milk as an acceptable drink, milk is not necessarily the best source of calcium for several reasons:

1. All milk in the United States has been treated by homogenization, pasteurization, and other processes that kill the enzymes and bacteria that make the calcium digestible and bioavailable for our bodies.
2. These treatments change the pH of the milk, which inhibits the calcium from being absorbed.
3. Most importantly, the Bible forbids the consumption of milk and meat at the same time, which most Americans do not practice.

The scientific explanation of why the Bible forbids this food combination is that excess protein consumption prevents calcium absorption. So drinking milk with a heavy meat meal will render the calcium to become functionally useless. (As little as 5 percent is absorbed in these situations.) Therefore, it is important to eat lots of leafy green vegetables such as Brussels sprouts, kale, mustard greens, broccoli, bok choy, and cauliflower. These vegetables have upwards of 50 percent absorption rate of calcium, which is about ten times what a milk and meat meal would provide. When incorporated daily, these vegetables can dramatically improve the calcium levels in the body.

POTASSIUM

Potassium, an extremely important and underrated mineral, is used in every cell of the body, especially in the brain, nerves, heart, muscles, and blood. Potassium uses its positive electrical charge as an electrical pump to push water and nutrients into cells and waste out of cells. This is why it is called an "electrolyte." It is vitally important for maintaining homeostasis, or balance, in the body.

Deficiency in potassium causes muscle cramping or weakness, swelling and fluid retention, and irritability. More severe cases of potassium deficiencies include nerve problems, confusion, irregular heartbeats, kidney stones, and high blood pressure. Ironically, diuretic medications for high blood pressure remove sodium and potassium from the body. Therefore, these drugs can control the blood pressure problem but can cause other symptoms to worsen. A medical supervisor should seriously monitor potassium supplementation if you suffer from kidney disease or take diuretics, as it can disrupt the effects of these diseases and medications.

Potassium is found in almost every plant food, so it is difficult to miss if you are eating a biblical diet. The absolute best sources of potassium are bananas, oranges, cantaloupes, tomatoes, potatoes, lima beans, avocados, and garlic. Since potassium is an electrolyte, it gets excreted, or exits the body, through sweat. Therefore, more should be consumed if you are sweating a lot. This is why potassium is added to a lot of sports drinks. The recommended daily intake for potassium is between 1.9 and 5.6 grams depending upon activity level.

SODIUM

Sodium, one of the most important minerals in the body, works with potassium as its antagonist (opposite) in cells in the body. Together, these two maintain water and nutrient levels in the cells through a mechanism called the "sodium-potassium pump." In this pump, sodium molecules outside of the cell are traded for potassium molecules inside the cell. This allows fluid and nutrients to be passed through the cell wall.

Sodium and potassium must be balanced with each other in order to function properly. The problem with the standard American diet is that most people eat two to three times more sodium than necessary while consuming less than normal potassium. This leads to a severe imbalance in the body, which causes fluid retention problems, high blood pressure, and muscle and nerve problems.

Due to this problem, sodium must be treated differently than other minerals. Sodium levels should be knowingly limited in order to balance the sodium-potassium ratio. The ideal intake is between 1,500 to 2,300 milligrams per day.

ZINC

Zinc, an essential mineral that is most commonly known for boosting the immune system, is also necessary for healthy reproductive organs. It contributes to proper memory function by helping neurotransmitter transportation. It is used in the brain, muscles, bones, kidneys, liver, and even the eyes. Actually it is used for DNA gene expression in every cell of the body. It behaves as an antioxidant and a powerful protective agent with studies demonstrating it has the ability to improve heart disease.[72]

An inadequate amount of zinc in the body increases chances of many diseases, including prostate cancer, cardiovascular disease, impaired growth and development in children, and cognitive impairment.[73] The recommended daily value for zinc is 11 milligrams. Approximately two billion people worldwide are deficient in zinc.[74]

Some signs of low zinc in the body include loss of taste, smell, and appetite; rough, dry skin and hair; dandruff; slow wound healing; or poor immune system (get sick easily).

One of the best methods for testing zinc at home is called a "zinc challenge." In a zinc challenge, you put a tablespoon of liquid zinc in your mouth, swish it around, and then swallow it. If the zinc has no taste, then your body is deficient in zinc. If the liquid is metallic and distasteful, then your body contains adequate zinc. This is an interesting design feature that God created to prevent humans from overdosing on zinc, which is toxic.

Zinc sulfate is the most common supplement form because it is the cheapest to produce. Unfortunately zinc sulfate is also the least absorbable. Zinc citrate is much more bioavailable for the body and is the recommended supplemented form. If you exhibit low zinc in a zinc challenge, supplement zinc daily and retest weekly until your body demonstrates adequate zinc levels.

Zinc is the most available in natural foods that God designed for us to eat: fish, fowl, eggs, pumpkin seeds, sunflower seeds, sesame seeds, poppy seeds, black currant, and other nuts and seeds. Zinc that is found in processed, synthetic foods (e.g., fortified cereals) is not bioavailable because it is bound to anti-nutrients, which prevent it from being absorbed.

CHROMIUM

Chromium is a trace element that is vital for blood sugar regulation because it helps transport sugar from the blood into the cell. The standard American lifestyle has been known to deplete chromium because it involves high sugar diets and sedentary habits. In addition, antacids, which a fourth of all Americans use regularly, reduce chromium absorption. As a result, many Americans do not have enough chromium.

The recommended daily allowance for chromium intake is between 50 and 200 micrograms. Chromium is found in the highest concentrations in broccoli, grapes, potato skins, spices, red meat, and other vegetables that have been grown in fertile soil. Chromium also increases in foods cooked in stainless-steel cookware. Chromium absorption is enhanced with vitamin C and niacin (vitamin B3), which is why vegetables raised in fertile soil is the ideal source for chromium. The most absorbable form of chromium in supplement form is chromium picolinate.

COPPER

Copper is a trace element used for many different processes such as cellular energy, oxygen transport, nerve transmission, healing and tissue repair, red blood cell production, and much more. In fact, it plays such an important part in cellular health and reproduction that babies are born with four times more copper than adults.[75]

Before modern medicine, copper was used as an antiseptic as well as to treat ulcers, accelerate wound healing, reduce eczema, and even treat venereal diseases during Roman times. Most of the ancient medical applications of copper appear to be topical. This seems to agree with modern scientific data as well. Transdermal (through the skin) copper has been shown in some current medical literature to be effective at reducing the effects of arthritic pain.

German physician Werner Hangarter first studied this phenomenon in 1939. He observed that copper miners throughout Europe were immune to arthritis while the rest of the continent was suffering from an arthritis epidemic. He later developed successful medical trials and copper-based treatments for rheumatoid arthritis, rheumatoid fever, neck and back pain, and sciatica. This is the basis behind all of the copper arthritis bracelets, bands, and wearable copper items sold in stores today.

Copper was also used throughout the Bible. In fact, it is mentioned more than any other metal: 148 times in 125 verses. In the temple, God commanded that all of the utensils be formed out of copper for the priests to use. In addition, the columns outside of the entrance of the temple were to be made of copper along with the clasps, sockets, rings, posts, and other parts of the enclosures. This was to provide health benefits to the priests while spiritually symbolizing the flawed nature of humanity. The copper was juxtaposed to gold, which symbolized purity of God, and was inlayed inside the ark of the covenant and the inner dwelling place of God.

Copper deficiency in the United States is rare. People who are at a higher risk for copper deficiency include premature infants, persons with malabsorption syndromes, and individuals who have had gastric bypass surgery (those struggling to digest their food properly). The proper intake for copper is 1 to 3 milligrams a day for adult men and women. Copper overdose is also extremely rare in the United States, but it can be toxic. Copper competes with zinc in the body, and the proper ratio of copper to zinc is one-to-ten.

IODINE

Iodine is one of the most important minerals for our body because it is essential for thyroid function. The thyroid controls the metabolism and growth of all cells in the body via the thyroid hormones, which are made of iodine molecules. These thyroid hormones are known as triiodothyronine (or T3 because it has three iodine molecules attached) and thyroxine (or T4 because it has four iodine molecules). Because they control cellular metabolism, they affect every physiological system in our bodies: breathing, heart rate, brain function, muscle strength, menstrual cycles, cholesterol levels, and so on.

Mild thyroid dysfunction usually manifests as mental and physical fatigue, cold hands and feet (low body temperature), swelling due to poor circulation, unexplainable weight gain, excessive hair loss, and possible nagging infections (since the immune system is impaired). Severe thyroid dysfunction can cause a goiter, an enlargement of the thyroid gland in the throat. Severe thyroid dysfunction can also lead to depression and intellectual decline. In fact, iodine deficiency is the leading cause of preventable intellectual disabilities in children.[76]

The RDA values for iodine intake in the United States are 160 milligrams a day for both men and women. The United States has been adding iodine to salt for the past century, which has reduced iodine deficiencies substantially. Yet despite proper access to iodized salt, the American Thyroid Association estimates that approximately 20 million Americans suffer from thyroid dysfunction and an estimated 60 percent of people are unaware of their condition.[77]

The biggest factor causing an increase in thyroid dysfunction over the past few decades is not a lack of iodine, but an increase in synthetic, toxic chemicals that prevent iodine from being utilized. The two biggest culprits are perchlorate and halide poisoning.

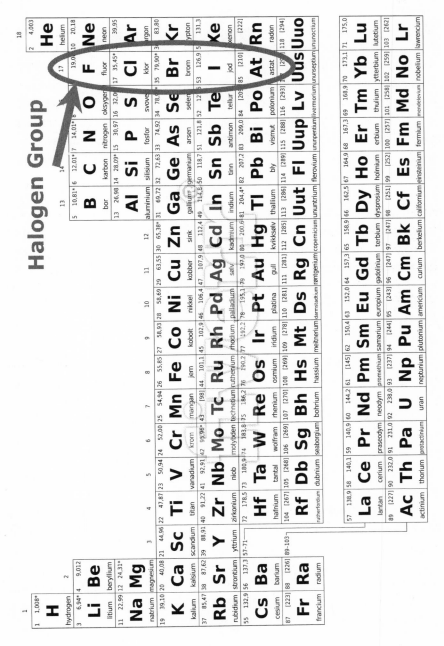

In halide poisoning, elements from the halogen group of the periodic table get into our bodies and bind to the thyroid hormones where iodine should have been bound. This changes the composition of the hormones and makes them unusable by the body. Halide poisoning occurs because halogen elements appear on the periodic table in the same column as iodine, which means they all share the same electrical charge of -1. They have the same chemical reaction patterns as each other and are easily interchangeable with each other. They are comparable to the way that all American electrical plugs work with all American electrical sockets, even though different appliances serve different purposes.

Unfortunately, halide poisoning is difficult to detect because these false thyroid hormone molecules behave very similarly to the real ones. In fact, they even fool most thyroid tests with false negatives. (They appear normal.) However, they do not function properly at all. This is problematic if it occurs in large quantities because the body will start to manifest as having an underactive thyroid, or hypothyroidism, due to the lack of functional hormones being produced. Here is an example of a malfunctioning T3 thyroid hormone, which has had its iodine replaced by either chlorine, fluorine, or bromine:

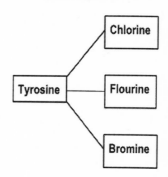

Active T3 Hormone = Tyrosine + 3 Iodines

Malfunctioning T3 Hormone

This is becoming more widespread because both chlorine and fluoride are added to our water systems, and bromine is used more and more every day for home and industrial uses. As these chemicals pervade our society, we will see an increase in unexplainable thyroid problems due to malfunctioning thyroid hormones.

The second major culprit behind iodine-related health problems in the United States is perchlorate, a synthetic chemical that is used industrially as propellants in rockets, fireworks, explosives, ammunitions, and so on. Perchlorate blocks the body's ability to uptake or absorb iodine into the thyroid gland. In fact, the pharmaceutical industry has used perchlorate to treat overactive thyroids for years (to lower it to normal).

Unfortunately, perchlorate is water-soluble and has been so widely produced that it has infiltrated most of the water supply across the globe. As a result, it has been tested and discovered in many farms, crops, animals, people, and so forth. It has even been discovered in many "organic" foods at the supermarket. Traces of perchlorate have been discovered in just about every human tested. I believe this is why we have started to observe a widespread increase in thyroid problems and iodine deficiency symptoms even though there is an adequate supply of iodine in our diet.

Fortunately, God designed our bodies to dispel toxins; therefore, these types of low-level poisonings do not have to last forever. There are two things we can do to assist in removing both perchlorate and excess halides from our bodies. The first thing we must do is severely restrict our exposure to these toxins. The most common sources of bromine include:

- Plastics (especially if they are off-gassing such as new cars, new water bottles, etc.)
- Freshly printed receipt paper
- Rubber/plastic surface cleaning chemicals
- Flame retardants
- Surfaces of printed circuits (computer parts)
- Some medicines
- Batteries
- Oil drilling liquids
- Some pesticides
- Some hair styling products
- Some food preservatives

The second-most important thing that we can do to improve our thyroid function and increase our iodine utilization is to eat multi-cationic salts, which are sea salts or Himalayan salts. Unlike regular table salt, these multi-cationic salts are loaded with trace minerals that can neutralize the halide chemicals in our bodies.

Then as we consistently do these two prescribed things (removing the unnatural chemical burden and replacing it with healthy trace minerals from natural salts), our body's innate detoxification systems can perform its work without being overburdened, our bodies can naturally heal themselves as God designed, and we can begin to develop the healthiness that God designed for us to have from the beginning.

SULFUR

Sulfur is another essential mineral for our bodies. In nature, it is easily identified for the way it burns. It creates a liquid fire with an irritating odor, invoking the sight and smell of volcanic ash. (It is a common element found in lava.) In the Bible, it is mentioned as brimstone (literally "smoking rock") and written as an idiom for God's wrath. For example, in Genesis 19:24, the Bible says that God poured out the wrath of "fire and brimstone" on the cities of Sodom and Gomorrah for their exceeding wickedness. In Psalm 11:6 (NASB), it says, "upon the wicked God will rain snares: fire and brimstone and burning wind will be the portion of their cup."

In biology, sulfur must become bonded to a carbon molecule, which turns it into an organic molecule in order for the body to utilize it. Some examples of organic sulfur are methylsulfonylmethane (MSM) and sulforaphane glucosinolate (SGS). Organic sulfur compounds are powerful antioxidants, and they are necessary for healthy arteries and veins. They help regulate blood sugar. They are vital components for collagen, the substance that gives elasticity to tendons, ligaments, and skin. Sulfur is involved in the composition of hormones, enzymes, and even antibodies. Therefore, sulfur is necessary for the entire body and is most necessary for the immune, cardiovascular, hormonal, and nervous systems. Studies have demonstrated that sulfur fights against cancer cells and protects healthy cells against the adverse effects of harsh cancer treatments such as chemotherapy.[78] Therefore, a lack of sulfur can lead to many health problems. Scientists believe that low sulfur will increase the risk of obesity, heart disease, Alzheimer's, chronic fatigue, and much more.[79]

Unfortunately petrochemical fertilizer farms have reduced the bioavailability of sulfur in our food supply because they spray inorganic (not carbon bound and not available to the body) sulfurs onto crops to increase yields. Therefore, many of the plants grown in these fields do not have adequate bioavailable sulfur. This is another example of how unnatural chemicals are harming the natural foods that God gave us for our healthiness. Absolute sulfur deficiency is rare, yet most people are on the low end of normal and nowhere near the excessively healthy amount of sulfur. So it is important to avoid petro-fertilized farm foods by eating organically, growing your own garden, and especially avoiding processed foods altogether. (Preprocessed foods are the lowest quality crops with the most amount of synthetic alterations.)

The best natural sources of sulfur are onions, garlic, dark leafy vegetables, kale, and broccoli. Secondarily, nuts, wild-caught seafood, and grass-fed meats contain adequate amounts of sulfur.

SELENIUM

Selenium, another trace mineral that is vital to health, is a non-metal element on the periodic table. Within our bodies, it functions as a powerful antioxidant. It is especially useful for reproductive organs, thyroid, immune system, and even DNA. One meta study (a published research paper that analyzes all research for a certain topic) concluded that an increase in selenium is related to a decrease in prostate cancer risk. It has also been associated with stronger sperm count and greater sperm motility.

However, selenium deficiencies are associated with an increased risk of dying from all causes. This means that people who are low in selenium are more likely to die from other pathological condition, even if selenium deficiency were not the cause of the illness to begin with. Selenium works best when paired with vitamin E. Most people have adequate selenium, although smoking, drinking, long-term birth control, stress, and malabsorption syndromes all cause selenium to become depleted in the body. Also more is needed when the immune system gets suppressed (e.g., when you get sick).

The recommended daily values for selenium are 55 micrograms a day. This is a very small amount. The best sources of selenium include fish, garlic, grains, seeds, and nuts. Overprocessing and refining foods will destroy the bioavailability of selenium. Therefore, it is important to include a variety of natural, God-designed plant foods to ensure that your selenium levels are adequately maintained. Selenium is safe to supplement if necessary.[80]

MANGANESE

Manganese is another trace mineral that doesn't get much attention but is essential for our health. It is used in such small quantities that there is no

RDA for it. However, it is necessary for strong bones and the utilization of B1. Given that most Americans do not have proper utilization of B1, it is safe to say that we all could use more manganese. Studies have shown that it can improve osteoporosis (weak bones) when taken in conjunction with calcium, zinc, and copper for over a year. The amounts used in the study were: 5 milligrams manganese, 1,000 milligrams of calcium, 15 milligrams of zinc, and 2.5 milligrams of copper.[81] This is significant because osteoporosis rates continue to climb in the United States every year.[82]

Manganese, like the other metals, is toxic to the brain in large quantities, so it should not be megadosed or megasupplemented. Manganese can be obtained from plant-based foods grown in nutrient-rich soils, the way God designed it to be.

CHLORIDE

Chloride is an essential mineral that is primarily used as an electrolyte in the body, due to its -1 electrical charge. Therefore, it opposes +1 charged electrolytes. (They work together like positive and negative on a battery.) Together, electrolytes control things like electrical conductivity of the nerves, fluid levels in the tissue, and acid/base balance in the cells. Chloride is especially important because it helps control the electrical pulsing of the heart and the utilization of GABA, a major neurotransmitter.

Chloride deficiency is rare, although it can be life-threatening when it does occur. Chloride intake usually occurs through salt (NaCl). Also we chlorinate our water supply to kill germs. As a result of these two things, most Americans actually have too much chloride that increases fluid retention and causes high blood pressure. Our bodies are designed to dispose of excess chloride through our urine, and our bodies naturally monitor our electrolyte levels. This is why high blood pressure seemingly only appears in people later in life. Chloride does not generally need to be supplemented. If anything, we need to try to limit our levels of chloride. It is also a culprit in the phenomenon known as "halide poisoning," which was described in the iodine section of this book.

In halide poisoning, the halide elements such as chloride and fluoride will displace iodine in the body and create thyroid malfunction. This is difficult to detect because it fools normal thyroid tests. Therefore, I generally recommend replacing table salt with natural sea salts or Himalayan salts as well as purifying your water to displace the excess chloride and fluoride. And I definitely do not recommend supplementing chloride under normal circumstances unless warranted by blood work or endorsed by your health professional for your specific circumstances.

PHOSPHORUS

Phosphorus, one of the most abundant minerals in the body, is primarily used for strong bones and teeth and secondarily for tissue growth and repair. Deficiency in phosphorus can cause a host of problems involving the bones, the brain, and digestion. Symptoms of low phosphorus include frail bones, stiff joints, bone pain, fatigue, anxiety, irritability, appetite loss, weight fluctuations, and so on. Phosphorus deficiency is rare in First World countries. In fact, phosphorus deficiencies are usually only caused by nutrient digestion problems (e.g., Crohn's or celiac disease), medications that cause you to leak electrolytes (e.g., diuretics), or kidney problems (since kidneys filter electrolytes out of the body).

The bigger problem in the United States is eating the right type of phosphorus. Most of the phosphorus found in the US food supply is not the right type. The correct type of phosphorus is organic because it is attached to a carbon molecule. This type is easily digested and used throughout the body. Inorganic phosphorus is not bound to a carbon molecule and cannot be used in the body. Unfortunately inorganic phosphorus is used throughout the food processing industry as a flavor enhancer. It is found in almost every soft drink as phosphoric acid. Therefore, most Americans, who eat a diet high in processed foods and soft drinks, will test normal for phosphorus but in fact have many of the signs and symptoms of low phosphorus.

One of the best ways to reverse this trend is to remove processed drinks from the diet. Water, teas, and coffees are substantially healthier for the body in the long run. In addition, processed foods should be removed from the diet and replaced with naturally occurring foods grown in nutrient-rich soils.

Eating from a garden can also improve organic phosphorus intake. Lastly, make sure your garden is fertilized naturally. You want to use manure or compost instead of synthetic chemicals on your plants. This is substantially healthier for your soil, plants, and body. And interestingly, it is the way God designed food to be grown in the first place!

MOLYBDENUM

Molybdenum, a trace mineral, is necessary for breaking down sulfites and other metals and enzymes in the body. Therefore, a deficiency in molybdenum will make a person more susceptible to sulfite allergies. Sulfites exist as a preserving agent in many wines, cheeses, and meats. They aren't healthy to begin with, but lacking molybdenum causes our system to be unable to detoxify them from our bodies and will create a food sensitivity/allergy to sulfites.[83]

Molybdenum is also used to break down other metals and enzymes in the body. People with low molybdenum will also have harsher reactions to other toxins besides just sulfites and sulfates. Therefore, if you suffer from many food allergies, you may need to consider supplementing molybdenum.

Molybdenum also affects other areas of the body. Because it is involved in detoxification, molybdenum deficiencies will also increase risk of certain cancers such as esophageal cancer.[84] In addition, low molybdenum also leads to problems breaking down uric acid, a byproduct of digestion and cellular turnover, in the body. Uric acid is usually filtered out by the kidneys and excreted in the urine. Uric acid that is not removed fast enough will accumulate in large quantities in the joints. This causes an arthritis known as gout.

Therefore, people with low molybdenum are more likely to get gout. Gout primarily attacks the big toe but can affect any joint in the body. It causes pain, swelling, and an inability to move the affected joint freely. Fortunately, there is a very good natural remedy for getting rid of uric acid— drinking natural, pure cherry juice (unsweetened and unprocessed). Also, eating cherries helps, but you need to eat a lot of them. Cherries contain molybdenum and a powerful antioxidant phytonutrient, anthocyanins. Together, these compounds quickly neutralize uric acid.

I have written in a previous section about the God-given potency of phytonutrients in fighting diseases, and this is a perfect example. God created cherries because they taste delicious and they contain a divine combination of vitamins, minerals, and phytonutrients to combat gout and other disease processes.

With regard to molybdenum, the recommended daily values are 45 micrograms a day. The best sources of molybdenum are plant foods grown in fertile soils. The best types of foods are beans, lentils, and peas. A diet high in processed and artificial foods will be less likely to contain adequate molybdenum, another reason why Western culture is suffering from high food allergy and disease rates.

God's diet was designed with optimal nutrition for our bodies and can contain upwards of 100 micrograms of molybdenum daily. If you are suffering from the symptoms of low molybdenum, it is safe to supplement at between 50 to 1,500 micrograms per day. If you consume more than 1,500 micrograms per day (thirty times the normal dose), it can become toxic: it can cause hallucinations, heavy metal poisoning, copper imbalances (since it is used for copper metabolism), and even death. Although there have been almost no reported deaths from molybdenum overdoses in the past century, it is still important to recognize that it is a heavy metal and should not be supplemented in extreme amounts over long periods of time.

FLUORIDE

Fluoride is an interesting trace element to discuss. It is absolutely necessary for strong bones and teeth, in small quantities. The RDA is between 3 to 4 milligrams a day. However, most Americans consume far too much fluoride because it is added to every municipal water supply in America to reduce the amount of dental cavities in our society. Unfortunately it also dramatically increased our exposure to fluoride in unnatural amounts. This increases our risk of chronic fluoride poisoning. In excessive amounts, fluoride is quite toxic to the body, as it actually creates an opposite effect than intended. It softens bones and teeth! In addition, it poisons the brain, lowers IQ, permanently damages the kidneys and other organs, and inhibits thyroid hormone production.

In a study of animal populations, elk in the Madison-Firehole area of Yellowstone National Park had a 27 percent shorter life span than their genetically identical brethren in other parts of the world. They attributed the shortened life span to excessive fluoride exposure from the geyser. The researchers observed the elk to have unhealthily softened bones and teeth and weakened bodies. They were more susceptible to the harshness of winter, to malnourishment, and to becoming easier prey for predators. Ultimately, none of the elk from this region lived a normal, healthy life span.[85]

There have been multiple studies performed on humans using fluoride as treatment for osteoporosis (softening of bones), and the results have all been disastrous. In every study, the people who took fluoride got worse, had more fractures, and had more severe fractures. One study noted a threefold increase in fractures, and one study noted a direct correlation of fluoride ingestion and hip fractures due to rapid bone loss.[86]

Contrary to popular knowledge, America is actually one of the very last countries that still fluoridates their water supply. Most First World countries stopped fluoridating their public water supplies decades ago based on all of the research. Japan and 97 percent of Western European countries do not fluoridate their water and have no more cavities than the United States.

Based on this data, it would be safe to assume that most Americans consume a dangerous level of fluoride. As expected, studies performed by the CDC indicate that over 40 percent of United States teenagers exhibit softening of teeth based on excess fluoride exposure (a condition medically known as fluorosis).[87]

Therefore, I strongly suggest that excess fluoride be avoided. Obviously ingesting small amounts found in the soil and plant foods is healthy and acceptable. Topical fluoride found in toothpaste is necessary. However, I would strongly recommend drinking filtered water and avoiding all municipal tap water in the United States. In addition, I recommend following some of our detoxification methods mentioned later in this book to help the body flush out excessive heavy metals, like fluoride, from the body.

ENZYMES

One of the most important and least studied aspects of our diets and our health are enzymes. Enzymes are made mostly from proteins (although a few are complex carbs), and they control chemical reactions in living things. In other words, they stimulate the chemical reactions in our bodies to occur in the same way that a coach teaches his or her team how to win but doesn't actually step on the field to play the game. Some examples of enzyme-assisted processes are breaking down the food we eat, creating hormones, building cellular components, duplicating DNA, or extracting energy from energy molecules. There are trillions of chemical reactions happening every day, which are absolutely necessary for life, and enzymes affect them all.

Enzymes can make the chemical reactions happen more easily or more difficult (to prevent bad ones from happening) or allow chemical processes to occur circumstantially (e.g., preventing hormones from being produced if you have too much of that hormone). They function by altering the equation of the chemical reaction—to change the heat capacity of a reaction, to change the amount of energy needed to create a chemical reaction, to change the time it takes for a reaction to occur, to change the concentration of chemicals needed to react together, and so on and so forth. An example of the function of an enzyme would be like adding salt to water so it boils faster. There are over 3,000 known enzymes in our bodies and an estimated 50,000 undiscovered/unstudied enzymes.

One of the most famous examples of an enzyme is CoQ10, or coenzyme Q10. CoQ10 is a fat-soluble compound that helps with energy production within cells and works as an antioxidant in the energy production cycle by preventing fats from being broken up into damaging free radicals. It also regenerates other antioxidants such as vitamins C and E and has been shown to enhance their antioxidant properties by making them more effective. And while CoQ10 is the most famous enzyme in the body, it is not the only enzyme in our body, and the others are just as important as CoQ10 for our health.

Sadly, most dietary enzymes are heat-labile, which means heat destroys them. This is unfortunate because it means when we cook food, we destroy most of the enzymes in the food that God created for us to have. This also means we destroy enzymes when we pasteurize and homogenize our dairy products. This could have significant medical consequences, as we do not yet fully understand how valuable these dietary enzymes are for our bodies.

This is a newer and less understood area of health, but multiple studies are emerging that demonstrate a direct correlation between enzyme deficiencies and chronic illnesses. While correlation doesn't prove causation (that the enzyme deficiency causes the pathology, as opposed to the pathology causing the enzyme deficiency), it does show us, scientifically speaking, that we need more dietary enzymes one way or another if we are dealing with chronic degenerative diseases.

Fortunately God's food has a plethora of enzymes built into it, and when we eat it in its raw form, we can enjoy all of the benefits (known or unknown) that His diet has for us. This is another example of why God's diet of raw fruits, vegetables, seeds, and nuts is so amazingly powerful for healing us, preventing disease, and creating longevity of life.

FIBER

Dietary fiber is another important, but often ignored, aspect of our food. Fiber has a vast array of health benefits, and by design, it is found almost exclusively in plant foods. Dietary fiber consists of very large molecules (cellulose and pectin from plants) that humans do not digest or absorb due to their size and the lack of enzymes to break them down. Therefore, fiber creates bulk in the stool, which contributes to a healthy environment in our digestive tracts.

Surprisingly, much of our healthiness begins with the digestive tract. In addition, the digestive tract is a strong reflector of our overall health. In other words, if we are often having major health problems in other areas, our digestive tract is also having major health problems. This is because the digestive tract actually does a lot more than simply absorb nutrients. It has many other purposes for our health, which most people do not realize.

For example, we have a tremendous amount of immune system tissue in our intestines, which react to the food we eat. When we eat food that is foreign to our bodies, such as toxins, it creates an inflammatory response within the body that lasts until we expel that food. This is why our diet is so significant in affecting autoimmune diseases and why it is so important to return to the food that God designed for us for healthy immune function.

In addition, the intestinal tract also has its own nervous system called the enteric nervous system. It is sometimes called the "second brain" because it has more nerve connections than anywhere in the peripheral nervous system or spinal cord! Some people attribute this second brain with providing us with a gut feeling about situations we encounter. And even though the enteric nervous system doesn't think like our first brain, it does contribute to mood, so much so that 95 percent of our primary feel-good neurotransmitters, or serotonin, are found in the intestines.

Research suggests that this second brain also regulates many other functions in the body, such as bone density, which is why it is of utmost importance to keep the intestinal tract and its second brain healthy.

The primary purpose of fiber is to keep the intestinal tract healthy. The primary source of fiber is natural, unprocessed plant foods. Fiber does several things to keep the intestines healthy:

1. Increase the volume and density of the stool, making it fuller, softer, and easier to pass through the intestines
2. Regulate the motility of the stool by either speeding it up or slowing it down (depending upon the type of fiber) so we have a consistent absorption of nutrients

In other words, it regulates bowel speed from being too extreme (such as diarrhea on one end of the spectrum to severe constipation on the other). This has many other wonderful side effects such as stabilizing blood sugar levels, helping us feel full after eating, preventing dehydration, and so forth.

Another extremely important purpose of fiber is that it feeds the healthy bacteria within the digestive tract, which contains millions of living bacterial cells that have a symbiotic, mutually beneficial relationship with us. They produce B vitamins for us as well as vitamin K2. They also generate other chemicals that we can use. They also occupy valuable real estate that prevents bad bacteria from moving in, taking over, and making us sick. There are many mutually beneficial aspects to the relationship we have with the bacteria in our guts, and there are many inflammatory and autoimmune diseases that occur when this relationship becomes dysfunctional. Therefore, it is extremely important to feed the bacteria with a healthy supply of fiber because, of all of the reasons above, fiber is one of the most crucial elements of our diet.

In fact, it affects far more than simple intestinal health. A high fiber diet is directly related to a reduction in all-cause mortality for all diseases. Studies show that a high fiber diet has been shown to lower risk of heart disease by 40 percent. It also reduces the risk of diverticulitis by 40 percent. It also reduces risk of stroke by 7 percent for every 7 grams of fiber consumed daily. It reduces risk of gallstones, kidney stones, and hemorrhoids. A high fiber diet reduces the risk of gut dysbiosis (which we discussed earlier as the death of the healthy bacteria in the intestines). A high fiber diet improves acne by reducing intestinal yeast overgrowth and toxic output through the skin.

The list goes on and on, but the research is very clear. Fiber is extremely important to our health and is found only in plant foods that God designed for us to eat. In addition, the plants should be eaten with minimal processing in order to retain the fiber content and other nutritional value.

For example, juicing machines deliberately remove the fiber content from the fruit and vegetables so they are easier to consume. However, this defeats one of the greatest benefits of eating fruits and vegetables in the first place. Drinking only the juice simply concentrates the sugar content. Therefore, I strongly encourage blending over juicing because blending leaves the fiber content intact and allows for the proper sugar/fiber ratio.

Another unhealthy form of processing for most vegetables is heating. Heat breaks down fiber significantly. For example, a cooked carrot is softer and therefore less fibrous than a fresh carrot. So as a general rule, you should not overcook your vegetables to the point of mushiness because you will have destroyed most of the fiber content (although slightly cooked vegetables are acceptable).

In summary, fiber is a much-ignored, but extremely valuable, element of our diet. If we are going to truly live the life that God designed for us and enjoy the health that He designed for us to have, we must enjoy plant-based foods with an abundance of fiber.

HYDRATION

Hydration, or adequate water supply, is an important aspect of our diet that is commonly brushed aside for more seemingly important things. However, dehydration is a chronic problem in our society. Statistically speaking, 75 percent of Americans are chronically dehydrated, which means they habitually do not consume enough water. The human body is made up of 60 percent water with muscles being comprised of 85 percent water, brain and heart are 73 percent water, and lungs are 85 percent water. Therefore, maintaining an appropriate fluid level is absolutely important for health and life. Water is the base substance in which most of our chemical reactions occur.

In addition, water acts as a buffer for most of the chemical reactions in our bodies because it has a relatively neutral pH balance. This means it has a balanced electrical charge so it can bind to both positively- and negatively-charged molecules or atoms. On a larger scale, having appropriate and balanced water levels improves a host of functions such as digestion, absorption of nutrients, blood viscosity (how smooth blood flows), body temperature regulation, and even skin detoxification.

Studies show that appropriate water intake will increase the metabolic system (our ability to burn fat and lose weight) by 30 percent. It also secondarily encourages weight loss by decreasing appetite. Not having proper water levels can lead to a host of problems, such as muscle cramping, chronic constipation and digestion problems, skin breakouts, kidney problems (and kidney stones), and even more serious problems, depending upon the severity of the dehydration.

Not all scientists are in full agreement, but the generally accepted consensus among professionals is that you should drink half your body weight in ounces every day. That means that if you weigh 200 pounds, then you should drink 100 ounces of water every day.

Fortunately, God-designed foods contain ample amounts of water and contain it in perfect ratios with other nutrients to maximize its benefits (such as pH level). This allows us to eat foods that assist in the benefits of proper hydration without having to drink copious amounts of water and take restroom breaks every hour.

In fact, drinking too much water is also harmful, as it dilutes the mineral content in the body, but if you look at the food that God originally designed for us to eat (fresh, unprocessed fruits and vegetables), they contain anywhere from 60 to 92 percent water. This means that if you are eating the foods that God designed you to eat, you will never have to worry about being dehydrated or diluting your mineral levels. Modern scientists speculate that we should get 20 percent of our fluid levels from our food, but if you follow a strict vegetarian diet that is primarily comprised of fruits and vegetables (as opposed to processed grains or dairy products), you can get upwards of 40 percent of your daily water requirement straight from the food you eat.

And since this water is saturated with vitamins, minerals, enzymes, and all of the other elements we have already discussed, it is perfectly assimilated into our bodies and converted into long-term physical healthiness. This is why many professional athletes now drink coconut water as a replenishment drink as opposed to synthetic sports drinks. The ratio of carbs, electrolytes, and other nutrients are perfect for our bodies, easily digested, and otherwise perfectly designed to fuel our bodies for peak performance. In fact, there is not a more perfect way to get fluids than through the foods that God designed for us to eat.

God's diet, by design, includes an excellent and abundant source of natural fluids for our bodies. If you want to maintain the physique that He designed for you, you must include these water-rich foods into your diet. You would be surprised at how much younger, healthier, and more elastic your skin looks when you eat His designer foods. You will be shocked at the decrease in joint stiffness, muscle achiness, and other pains that occur at large in our society due to chronic dehydration. You will almost instantly begin to appreciate the youthfulness that occurs when you eat the foods that God designed for you and you begin to experience proper hydration.

MICROORGANISMS

The world is full of microbiological organisms such as viruses, fungi, and bacteria. These cellular organisms are vital for life on earth and can be either beneficial or severely damaging to our physical health. This is an important topic because there are actually ten times as many microorganisms in our bodies as there are human cells.[88] Under normal circumstances, these microorganisms provide nutrients to us that we could not create on our own without them.[89]

For example, our bodies are monogastric digesters by design, which means they have only one stomach chamber to break down foods. Therefore, they require bacteria in the intestines to aid in the digestive process. The bacteria break down food, create vitamin K2, and help absorb B vitamins. In addition, they aid in hormone regulation by recycling old hormones. Most importantly, they fight off bad microorganisms, which would make us sick, while also stimulating our immune system to fight bad microorganisms. They are so important that we could not be healthy without them. In fact, there are many autoimmune and inflammatory diseases associated with unhealthy intestinal microorganisms, and this is just one example of a microorganism in our bodies.

It is God's design for us to have a symbiotic (or mutually beneficial) relationship with these microorganisms, in a similar way that we are to have a symbiotic relationship with the other animals and plants. This comes from Genesis 1 when God commanded Adam and Eve to subdue the whole earth and have dominion over every living thing.

Another area where the Bible discusses microbiology (study of microorganisms) is when it speaks about leaven, a type of microorganism known as yeast, a single-celled type of fungus that is traditionally used in baking to make bread rise. This occurs because the yeast will feed on the simple sugars in dough, and after metabolizing it, it will expel carbon dioxide gases into the dough to create the holes in the bread.

Leaven is mentioned thirty-nine times throughout the Bible. Spiritually, leaven represents evil, corruption, or impurity. Throughout the Bible, God would command the Israelites to remove leaven from their foods and their homes for specific periods of time, such as the celebration of Passover, in order to cleanse themselves spiritually. This is where the modern Christian practice of passing unleavened bread for communion comes from.

Unfortunately, leaven, or yeast, is an antagonist to healthy bacteria in our bodies. They compete for the same nutrients in our intestines and the same territory within our bodies to settle down and colonize. And while healthy intestinal bacteria are beneficial for us, yeast is not. It has the opposite effect. First, it robs us of nutrition that we might otherwise need. Second, yeast metabolic waste and yeast cell death is toxic in large quantities. (This is known medically as a Herxheimer reaction.)

Therefore, yeast overgrowth is hugely problematic for our health. It is manageable in smaller quantities, but if it is used as the primary source of food in our diets, then it disrupts the natural order of microbial life that God designed. That is why the Bible uses yeast/leaven to represent impurity, corruption, evil, sin, and so on.

When God commanded the Israelites to remove leaven from their foods and houses during Passover, the command was dual-purposed. The first was to spiritually remind people to remove impurity from their lives and refocus on God. The second was to naturally restore healthy bacterial balance in the people. It would provide a time for the entire nation to purge themselves of yeast overgrowth and to restore the healthy bacteria in their bodies. This meant that while they were being obedient to God's spiritual laws, they were also healing their bodies. God's plan was for healing of his people in their totality—their spiritual nature, mental acuity, and physical health.

These biblical concepts speak volumes to our society today. The United States loves our yeast products, such as cakes, donuts, breads, desserts, and so forth. It is a major portion of our diet. This is largely reflected in our health statistics. Scientists estimate that 70 percent of Americans have candida (a family of yeast) overgrowth in their intestines, mouths, and/or skin.[90] In addition, half of all Americans suffer from allergies, 12 percent have recurring chronic sinus infections, and half of all sinus infections are fungal infections.[91]

The science is very clear: we have a serious yeast/fungal problem in America that needs to be addressed. Here are the most common signs of yeast/fungal overgrowth:

- Chronic bad breath
- Chronic abdominal pain, bloating, gas
- Itching, burning skin
- Itchy ears
- Adult acne
- Chronic allergies/sinus infections
- Chronic fatigue
- Chronic muscle and joint pain
- Chronic brain fog
- Strong cravings for starchy products
- Decreased immune system

Many of these fungal problems are further compounded by our irresponsible overuse of antibiotics, which only kill bacteria and do not affect yeast, fungi, or viruses. Doing this actually makes us more susceptible to fungal overgrowth because improperly prescribed antibiotics kill off our healthy bacteria and pave the way for fungal colonies to colonize.

In these instances, people get sick and then take a regimen of antibiotics. The antibiotics kill off the harmful bacteria but also destroy the healthy bacteria in the intestines. Then if nothing is done to replenish the healthy bacterial colonies, the microbial balance of their bodies is severely disrupted. Later, that person can start to develop symptoms of improper microbial health, such as the symptoms I listed above, because they never fully replenished their healthy intestinal bacteria. This problem can be compounded if this cycle is repeated multiple times.

I am not suggesting that people avoid medical doctor's prescriptions. I am recommending to supplement those regimens with healthy, probiotic foods in order to bolster the intestinal bacteria and prevent future fungal overgrowth and disease.

Fortunately, the Bible, though it was written thousands of years ago, offers specific advice on this subject. Many Bible verses speak about microbial management. These verses detail food preparation, hygiene, bathroom protocols, and many more lifestyle habits pertaining to microbial health. In the next two chapters, we will discuss internal microorganisms (in the food) and external microorganisms (in our environment) in detail. Both are equally important to our health and equally addressed by the Bible.

FERMENTED FOODS

Relating to our diets, there are two main ideas that come from the Bible: to routinely purge yeast/unhealthy microorganisms and to regularly eat healthily fermented foods. With regard to yeast/unhealthy microorganisms, we should completely remove them for at least one week (technically eight days according to the Bible) every year. During that time period, they should neither be in our foods nor our houses. This is important because the life span of a single yeast cell is just over a week. Normally they multiply over and over so a colony will last for weeks, months, or years. But if they are suppressed and cannot replicate, they will die out in a week or two (hence the weeklong usage when taking antifungal medications under normal circumstances).

During a biblical purge, or "fast," our bodies have the opportunity to normalize and rebalance our microorganisms, thus providing us with all of the health benefits mentioned earlier. I recommend that you practice this type of fast once a year.

Interestingly, in the book of Daniel, another country had captured Daniel and encouraged him to participate in their dietary practices. He insisted that God's plan was better. When they disagreed, he proposed a challenge. "Test your servants for ten days; let us be given vegetables to eat and water to drink. Then let our appearances be compared to those who have eaten the king's food, and deal with us according to what you see" (Daniel 1:12–13 NIV).

Much to the king's surprise and as a testimony to God's divine wisdom about our diets, Daniel and his men looked substantially healthier after the ten days and were allowed to continue to follow God's diet plan. Likewise, a yearly fast (or removal) from yeast will do seemingly miraculous things to your health.

The second idea about microorganisms in the Bible was to eat plenty of fermented foods, like yogurts, cheeses, wines, and fermented vegetables. These foods are loaded with healthy bacteria. When we eat them, the healthy bacteria go into our bodies and bolster the existing colonies of microorganisms to make us healthier. These fermented foods are mentioned all throughout the Bible as part of the normal dietary practice of that time period.[92] In fact, Jesus's first recorded miracle was turning water into wine (John 2:1–11), a fermented grape.

I also believe that manna from the Old Testament of the Bible was some type of fermented food. There were several times when God provided "manna from heaven" (Exodus 16:4) to feed the Israelites. It was never described, so no one truly knows what it is, but I believe it may have been a type of fermented food due to the nature of its description. It tasted sweet, it arrived only in the morning, it boosted the Israelites' health, it provided energy and nutrients, and it would sour by the end of the day.[93]

Before home refrigeration was invented, fermentation was used regularly throughout history to preserve food. Until the early 1900s, everyone on the planet ate fermented foods all of the time. It was a normal practice, not abnormal like it is today. Fermented foods can be made at home from scratch or from starter kits that already contain healthy bacteria in them. There are roughly five hundred strains inside our intestines. Most of these belong to four families: lactobacillus, bifidobacterium, saccharomyces, and streptococcus. If you choose to purchase probiotic supplements, look for these types. There should be a concentration of millions to billions so you can consume between one and ten billion daily, split up throughout the day.

There are many ways to cultivate fermented vegetables yourself without spending much money. The simplest and easiest is sauerkraut, which means "sour cabbage" in German. And although it is popular in historical German food, it has been eaten throughout the world in many civilizations for many years. If you have never fermented before, I recommend starting with it. Here is a basic recie:

Ingredients
1 head of fresh cabbage
3 tablespoons of salt
1 quart canning jar
Cheesecloth (or another breathable lid)

Directions
1. Slice cabbage into thin slices and place into jar.
2. Fill with water and salt until cabbage is completely submerged.**
3. Cover the lid of the jar with cheesecloth or other breathable lid.
4. Place jar of cabbage and brine in a low light, lower room temperature area.
5. Let it ferment for between two and fourteen days.*
6. After it is done fermenting, you can store it in the fridge or leave it out on the counter to continue fermenting.

* The longer the cabbage ferments, the stronger the taste and greater the number of probiotics. I recommend starting with less and working up your taste tolerance.
** Healthy bacteria is anaerobic, which means it doesn't breathe air. Therefore, cabbage must remain completely submerged in water at all times. If any bacteria grow on the surface of the water (i.e., it looks white, grey, green, or moldy), it must be skimmed off or discarded

SANITATION

The second aspect of proper microorganism health involves environmental microorganisms, or microorganisms outside our body. Having healthy environmental microorganisms is known as cleanliness and sanitation. Many Americans take sanitation for granted because it has been so deeply ingrained into our cultural identity. It could be argued that much of our prosperity is due to the longevity and productivity that comes as a result of proper sanitation. Many countries and cultures in the past and present do not practice the same level of sanitation and have not enjoyed the associated health and prosperity.[94] This is because so many of the microorganisms out in the environment have the potential to be seriously life-altering or even fatal.

God originally provided the cleanliness and sanitation laws to his people in order to prevent unhealthy microorganisms from spreading around and damaging our health. This is a subject in the Bible that gets almost no attention but is as significant as any other part of the Bible.

It can be observed that, as civilizations move farther away from biblical values, their sanitation tends to regress. For example, during the Dark Ages, people were highly religious and superstitious, but not biblical in practice. They had completely abandoned the sanitation laws. Sewage was left exposed in the streets, and rats lived in houses with people. These rats carried fleas that hosted an unhealthy microorganism called "Yersinia pestis." This microorganism caused the Black Plague, which was highly contagious and fatal. It spread from town to town, city to city, and country to country until it had wiped out approximately 30 to 60 percent of the world's entire population in just a few years.

Nearly five hundred years later, people began to abandon biblical sanitation laws again, this time involving medical practices. Deaths from infection during childbirth in hospitals rose to over 30 percent. During this time, doctors were going room to room without cleaning their tools, sanitizing their equipment, or washing their hands. As a result, they were carrying infections from one patient to another, even into the nurseries, and causing one in three children to pass away.

In 1845, Dr. Ignaz Philipp Semmelweis dedicated his life's research to this tragic phenomenon. Even though germs had not been discovered yet, Dr. Semmelweis observed that washing hands and tools dramatically reduced the infant mortality rate. He implemented and required handwashing for all of the doctors at all of his hospitals. The infant mortality rate was instantly reduced from 30 percent to less than 1 percent in those hospitals.

Because germ theory had not been discovered yet, he had no way to prove to his colleagues that the sanitation was causing the reduction in infant mortality rate. So the medical community rejected his theory about cleanliness and fired him. He died a martyr for sanitation, even though the Bible had prescribed it over two thousand years prior. It wasn't until the discovery of germs by Louis Pasteur years later that Semmelweis would receive the credit he was due for saving all of those children.

Similarly, as our culture departs from biblical principles, there is an observed neglection of our own sanitation. According to the CDC, handwashing compliance by medical doctors in hospitals is down to an all-time low of 40 percent.[95] And as a result, population studies show that the United States has the highest infant mortality rate of all OECD countries.[96] (OECD is the Organization for Economic Co-operation and Development, consisting of major First World countries.)

Fortunately, the Bible discusses sanitation at length. There are over eighty-three verses about sanitation in the Old Testament, covering a wide variety of topics. It would be too difficult to discuss each in complete detail in this book, but here is a table to summarize the most important points:

Isaiah 1:16 Isaiah 52:11	Keep yourself clean by washing yourself routinely.
Psalm 51:10	The use of antiseptics is recommended when washing. (Hyssop is a natural antiseptic.)
Ezekiel 36:25	Clean water should be used when washing.
Mark 7:3	Hands are to be washed before eating a meal.

Leviticus 13:45	People who are sick should cover their mouths when they communicate (and let others know they are sick).
Leviticus 14:8	People who are sick should wash their hands, clothes, and hair. They should wait seven days before socializing with others to ensure they don't spread disease. (This was written before they had sanitizing chemicals and would ensure the bacteria/virus was completely gone from their bodies.)
Numbers 5:1–3 Deuteronomy 23:12	Diseases should be avoided.
Leviticus 15:11	Wash your hands after being around someone who is sick.
Leviticus 15:5	Wash your hands, hair, and clothes after taking care of someone who is sick.
Leviticus 11:25	Wash your clothes after touching a carcass.
Deuteronomy 23:13	Relieving yourself should occur in a separate facility outside the place where normal activities take place.
Deuteronomy 23:13	Excrement should be buried in the ground or covered up completely.
Deuteronomy 23:16	Places of excrement should be avoided for normal daily activities.
Leviticus 15:1–13	Bodily fluids are considered unsanitary.
Leviticus 22:4–8	People with open sores or bodily fluids should not share food with others.
Deuteronomy 21:22–23	Dead bodies should be buried immediately.
Numbers 31:19–20	People who touch dead bodies should wash themselves and their clothes and tools.

There are many more verses about cleanliness and sanitation. Suffice it to say, it is important to keep ourselves and our environment clean and sanitary in order to prevent the spread of disease from unhealthy microorganisms. This is part of God's design for our lives, and it is imperative for biblical health.

SPIRITUAL HEALTH

The final aspect of our health is our spiritual health. We cannot become fully healthy without spiritual health because it is coupled with our mental and physical health. Yet, of the three, our spiritual health is most important. That is because our spirit is the most powerful and profound. It is the part of our nature that connects us to God. It is the very reason we were created, to communicate with and fully experience God. The spiritual nature of mankind is clearly demonstrated throughout the Bible. For example, in the very beginning, God walked with Adam and Eve on the earth in the garden of Eden (Genesis 3:8), then again with Enoch (Genesis 5:22–24) after the fall, and again with Noah (Genesis 6:9) before and after the flood. The Bible specifically shows us that God talks to people directly (Genesis 2:16, 3:9–19, 6:13) and that people talk directly back (Genesis 2:23, 3:10–19). This dialogue between mankind and God continues from that time until now, with each generation of people communicating with God and seeking His revelations to us. This is a demonstration of the manifestation of our spiritual nature. This is how we experience God.

Unfortunately, our spiritual "commlink" to God is broken and needs to be repaired. The Bible says that the original humans turned against God (or sinned), and as a result, their spiritual nature was damaged to the point of death, along with all of their offspring. Therefore, humans can no longer communicate with God freely without His intervention. As a result, we have been stripped of our ability to share His eternal scope of vision. In other words, we struggle to perceive anything other than our own immediate needs and wants. This has been scientifically observed throughout history and adequately described in the field of psychology. Psychologists have labeled this phenomenon as the "id, ego, and superego." This means that people, at their deepest levels, perceive the world exclusively through their own minds and care most about themselves.

Just analyze all of your thoughts for the past week and consider what subject matter has been of the most focus—yourself! This is unavoidable and our universal curse. We all wander aimlessly through life and fail to fully communicate to God or others because we are innately self-absorbed. We lack the ability to understand what God wants for us and therefore cannot fully live out His plan for us.

Unfortunately, this renders us unable to fulfill our mandate for our creation. In other words, we cannot completely be who we were created to be; nor do what we were created to do because we are so inwardly focused. The Bible calls this "falling short" or being "sinful in nature."[97] Our lives are not about counting good and bad things or striving for an acceptable behavior pattern. It is about communicating with God on the level He created us for, a task we cannot achieve on our own because we are spiritually sick and disconnected from God. Ultimately, if not healed, this spiritual sickness will lead to full spiritual death, a complete separation from God forever.

This spiritual separation from God is significant because God is the only true source of love (1 John 4:8), joy (1 Peter 1:8–9), peace (John 14:27), and everything that is good in the world, and His existence lasts forever (Psalm 107:1; James 1:17). In contrast, everything that is not from God will not last forever (Matthew 24:35). That is why spiritual healing is the most important healing we can receive. The Bible says in Matthew 16:26 (ESV), "For what will it profit a man if he gains the whole world and forfeits his soul? Or what shall a man give in return for his soul?"

Without spiritual healing, our very existence is painful and meaningless. Therefore, we unconditionally and critically need spiritual healing. Fortunately God is infinitely loving and capable. He sent spiritual healing to mankind by sending a part of Himself to us—His Son, Jesus Christ.

Jesus Christ came to earth from heaven to teach us about God's nature and to provide a means for us to be able to reconnect with God. He did this by dying in our place and taking our punishment for rebelling against God. He allowed Himself to be separated from God instead of us. He switched places with us so our spiritual nature could be healed. This was possible because God's Son, Jesus Christ, still had a fully intact spirit and could fully connect to God, experience God, and actualize His plan for His life. Jesus

Christ gave up His life for us, and His spirit (the Holy Spirit) was given to us in place of our own dying spirit (John 14:26) for anyone who seeks it (Luke 11:13).

Therefore, we can be spiritually healed by calling on the name of Jesus Christ. He said, "I am the way, the truth, and the life. No one comes to the father except through me" (John 14:6). Jesus offered salvation and eternal life to the entire world through His own sacrifice. And He asks every person on the planet into a repentant relationship with God. This means believing that Jesus is the Son of God, accepting His gift of salvation and denying your own selfish agenda. It is a simple prayer but begins a journey of newfound life and communication with God, which will last literally forever. It will continue far beyond this physical world into the next one, which will last for eternity.

CONCLUSION

My prayer for you is that through this book you may find healing, peace, joy, love, comfort, and all of the unlimited potentialities that can be found in life when lived under the blessings of God, His Son Jesus Christ, and the wonderful, natural world that we are commanded to steward. I pray that your heart is stirred and your soul is drawn to God. May you be encouraged to endure the trials, as the rewards are worth it. And may you be inspired to live the life worthy of the calling of Jesus Christ. May we spend eternity together praising His name. In conclusion, "I wish above all things that thou mayest prosper and be in health, even as thy soul prospereth" (3 John 1:2 KJV). God bless you.

For more information or to schedule online with
one of our health specialists, please visit our website:
www.DesignerDiet.org or www.DrMelot.Com.

REFERENCES

1   https://www.drugabuse.gov/sites/default/files/poppingpills-nida.pdf

2   National Institute on Drug Abuse, *America's Addiction to Opioids: Heroin and Prescription Drug Abuse* (2014).

3   https://ethics.harvard.edu/blog/new-prescription-drugs-major-health-risk-few-offsetting-advantages

4   U.S. Centers for Disease Control and Prevention

5   Alzheimer's Association, https://www.ncbi.nlm.nih.gov/pmc/articles/PMC 3026476/)

6   IMS Health

7   Depression and Bipolar Support Alliance

8   hrsa.gov/vaccinecompensation/data/index.html

9   Charles Seife, "Research Misconduct Identified by the US Food and Drug Administration," *MSI JAMA Intern Med*175(4)(2015):567–577, doi:10.1001/jamainternmed.2014.7774.

10 Karlie A. Intlekofer and Carl W. Cotman, "Exercise Counteracts Declining Hippocampal Function in Aging and Alzheimer's Disease," *Neurobiology of Disease* 57:47–55.

11 https://www.salk.edu/news-release/memory-capacity-of-brain-is-10-times-more-than-previously-thought/

12 https://www.ncbi.nlm.nih.gov/pmc/articles/PMC430793/

13 https://www.mayoclinic.org/healthy-lifestyle/infant-and-toddler-health/expert-answers/infant-growth/faq-20058037

14 http://www.industrytap.com/knowledge-doubling-every-12-months-soon-to-be-every-12-hours/3950

15 https://www.ncbi.nlm.nih.gov/pubmed/23222520

16 Living Planet Report, 2014.

17 https://www.ncbi.nlm.nih.gov/pmc/articles/PMC4707879/

18 American Society for Clinical Nutrition, "Vitamin C Elevates Red Blood Cell Glutathione in Healthy Adults" (1993).

19 W. Pöldinger, B. Calanchini, and W. Schwarz, "A Functional-Dimensional Approach to Depression: Serotonin Deficiency as a Target Syndrome in a Comparison of 5-hydroxytryptophan and Fluvoxamine," *Psychopathology* 24 (1991):53–81.

20 https://www.ncbi.nlm.nih.gov/pubmed/24606898

21 https://www.ncbi.nlm.nih.gov/pubmed/17868488

22 https://jamanetwork.com/journals/jamainternalmedicine/fullarticle/1696179

23 https://www.ncbi.nlm.nih.gov/pubmed/9437377

24 https://www.ncbi.nlm.nih.gov/pubmed/24625239

25 David J. A. Jenkins et al., "Effect of Lowering the Glycemic Load With Canola Oil on Glycemic Control and Cardiovascular Risk Factors: A Randomized Controlled Trial," *Diabetes Care* 37(7)(July 2014):1806–1814, https://doi.org/10.2337/dc13-2990.

26 Adam M. Bernstein, MD, ScD, Michael F. Roizen, MD, and Luis Martinez MD, MPH, "Purified Palmitoleic Acid for the Reduction of High-Sensitivity C-Reactive Protein and Serum Lipids: A Double-Blinded, Randomized, Placebo Controlled Study," *Journal of Clinical Lipidology* (August 19, 2014), DOI: https://doi.org/10.1016/j.jacl.2014.08.001.

27 G. Tsivgoulis et al., "Adherence to a Mediterranean Diet and Prediction of Incident Stroke," *Stroke* 46(3)(March 2015):780–785, doi: 10.1161/STROKEAHA.114.007894. Epub 2015 Jan 27.

28 Y. Gu et al., "Nutrient intake and plasma β-amyloid," *Neurology* 78(23)(June 5, 2012):1832–1840. doi: 10.1212/WNL.0b013e318258f7c2. Epub 2012 May 2.

29 L. G. Gillingham et al., "High-Oleic Rapeseed (Canola) and Flaxseed Oils Modulate Serum Lipids and Inflammatory Biomarkers in Hyper-cholesterolaemic Subjects," *J Nutr* 105(3)(Feb 2011):417–427. doi: 10.1017/S0007114510003697. Epub 2010 Sep 29.

30 https://www.canolacouncil.org/news/canola-and-high-oleic-canola-oils-reduce-belly-fat-in-adults/

31 Mary G. Enig, PhD, FACN, "Effects of Dietary Coconut Oil on the Biochemical and Anthropometric Profiles of Women Presenting Abdominal Obesity," *Lipids* 44(7)(July 2009):593–601. *Coconut: In Support of Good Health in the 21st Century*, http://coconutresearchcenter.org/

32 http://www.eurocbc.org/page483.html

33 https://www.cdc.gov/nchs/data/nhanes/databriefs/calories.pdf

34 https://www.michaeljfox.org/foundation/news-detail.php?Research-Suggests-Alzheimers-Type-3-Diabetes

35 A. L. Rosenbloom et al., "Emerging Epidemic of Type 2 Diabetes in Youth," *Diabetes Care* 22(2)(Feb 1999):345–354.

36 http://www.bmj.com/content/353/bmj.i2716

37 https://wholegrainscouncil.org/what-whole-grain

38 Z. S. El-Shamei et al., "A Comparison of the Effects of Three GM Corn Varieties on Mammalian Health," *Int J Biol Sci* 5(7)(2009):706–726, doi:10.7150/ijbs.5.706; Y. G. Ajeeb, "Histopathological Changes in Some Organs of Male Rats Fed on Genetically Modified Corn," *J Am Sci* 8(10)(2012): 684–696.

39 R. Mesnage et al., "Cytotoxicity on Human Cells of Cry1Ab and Cry1Ac Bt Insecticidal Toxins Alone or With a Glyphosate-Based Herbicide," *J Appl Toxicol* 33(2013): 695–699, doi:10.1002/jat.2712.

40 "Maternal and Fetal Exposure to Pesticides Associated to Genetically Modified Foods in Eastern Townships of Quebec," *Canada Reprod Toxicol.* 31(4)(May 2011):528–533, doi: 10.1016/j.reprotox.2011.02.004. Epub 2011 Feb 18.

41 https://www.ers.usda.gov/data-products/chart-gallery/gallery/chart-detail/?chartId=58340

42 K. H. Gabbay et al., "The Ascorbate Synthesis Pathway: Dual Role of Ascorbate in Bone Homeostasis," *The Journal of Biological Chemistry* (April 21, 2010).

43 Hsiao–Chi Wang et al., "Allyl Sulfides Inhibit Cell Growth of Skin Cancer Cells through Induction of DNA Damage Mediated G2/M Arrest and Apoptosis," *J Agric Food Chem* 58(11)(2010):7096–7103.

44 Carmia Borek, "Antioxidant Health Effects of Aged Garlic Extract," *Journal of Nutrition* 131(2001):1010S–1015S.

45 https://www.cdc.gov/nutritionreport/report.html; "Foods, Fortificants, and Supplements: Where Do Americans Get Their Nutrients?" *J Nutr* 141(10)(Oct 2011):1847–54, doi: 10.3945/jn.111.142257. Epub 2011 Aug 24.

46 American Association of Poison Control Centers, "Toxic Exposure Surveillance System 2004, Annual Report."

47 Bronstein et al., *Clinical Toxical* 49(10)(2011):910–941.

48 https://ethics.harvard.edu/blog/new-prescription-drugs-major-health-risk-few-offsetting-advantages

49 https://www.ncbi.nlm.nih.gov/pmc/articles/PMC5365188/

50 https://www.ncbi.nlm.nih.gov/pmc/articles/PMC2705821/

51 https://www.ncbi.nlm.nih.gov/pmc/articles/PMC3858911/

52 Mercola.com, "Vitamins That Reduce Your Risk of Skin Cancer."

53 E. Greco et al., "Reduction of the Incidence of Sperm DNA Fragmentation by Oral Antioxidant Treatment," *J Androl* 26 (3)(May-June 2005):349–353.

54 H. Henmi et al., "Effects of Ascorbic Acid Supplementation on Serum Progesterone Levels in Patients with a Luteal Phase Defect," *Fertility and Sterility* 80(2)(2003):459–461.

55 P. K. Myint et al., "Plasma Vitamin C Concentrations Predict Risk of Incident Stroke Over 10 y in 20 649 Participants of the European Prospective Investigation into Cancer Norfolk Prospective Population Study," *Am J Clin Nutr* 87(1)(2008):64–69.

56 Claire Doskey et al., "Tumor Cells Have Decreased Ability to Metabolize H2O2: Implications for Pharmacological Ascorbate in Cancer Therapy," *Redox Biology* 10 (2016):274–284. *PMC*. Web. 22 May 2017.

57 http://dx.doi.org/10.1016/j.ccell.2017.02.018

58 J. A. Wietzke and J. J. Welsh, "Phytoestrogen Regulation of a Vitamin D3 Receptor Promoter and 1,25-dihydroxyvitamin D3 Actions in Human Breast Cancer Cells," *Steroid Biochem Mol Biol* 84(2–3)(Feb 2003):149–157.

59 http://www.nutritionj.com/content/3/1/8

60 E. A. Klein et al., "Vitamin E and the Risk of Prostate Cancer. The Selenium and Vitamin E Cancer Prevention Trial," *JAMA* 306(14)(2011):1549–1556, doi:10.1001/jama.2011.1437; G. F. Combs, *Vitamin E. In the Vitamins: Fundamental Aspects in Nutrition and Health*, 2nd ed. (Academic Press, 1992), 190–219.

61 A. C. Allison, "The Possible Role of Vitamin K Deficiency in the Pathogenesis of Alzheimer's disease and in Augmenting Brain Damage Associated with Cardiovascular Disease," *Med Hypotheses* 57(2)(Aug 2001):151–155.

62 http://www.lifeextension.com/magazine/2004/3/aas/Page-01

63 J. Conly and K. Stein, "Reduction of Vitamin K_2 Concentrations in Human Liver Associated with the Use of Broad Spectrum Antimicrobials," *Clinical and Investigative Medicine* 17(6)(Dec 1944):531–539. PMID 7895417.

64 S. H. Zeisel and K. A. da Costa KA, "Choline: An Essential Nutrient for Public Health," *Nutrition Reviews* 67(11)(Nov 2009):615–623, doi:10.1111/j.1753-4887.2009.00246.x. PMC 2782876. PMID 19906248

65 http://www.who.int/nutrition/topics/ida/en/

66 J. Hunnicutt, K. He, and P. Xun, "Dietary Iron Intake and Body Iron Stores Are Associated with Risk of Coronary Heart Disease in a Meta-Analysis of Prospective Cohort Studies," *Journal of Nutrition* 144(3)(2014):359, doi: 10.3945/jn.113.185124.

67 https://doi.org/10.1093/jnci/djh047

68 http://dx.doi.org/10.1016/j.neurobiolaging.2014.03.039

69 Institute of Medicine, Food and Nutrition Board, "Dietary Reference Intakes: Calcium, Phosphorus, Magnesium, Vitamin D and Fluoride," (Washington, DC: 1997).

70 http://www.cnn.com/2014/12/31/health/magnesium-deficiency-health/index.html

71 *American Journal of Clinical Nutrition* 85(5)(May 2007):1361–1366.

72 https://www.ncbi.nlm.nih.gov/pubmed/20950764

73 https://www.ncbi.nlm.nih.gov/pmc/articles/PMC1125304/

74 https://www.ncbi.nlm.nih.gov/pmc/articles/PMC1125304/

75 A. Ralph and H. J. McArdle, *Copper Metabolism and Requirements in the Pregnant Mother, Her Fetus, and Children* (New York: International Copper Association, 2001).

76   http://www.who.int/nutrition/topics/idd/en/

77   https://www.thyroid.org/

78   https://doi.org/10.1016/j.tiv.2007.08.016

79   https://www.westonaprice.org/health-topics/abcs-of-nutrition/sulfur-deficiency/

80   http://www.umm.edu/health/medical/altmed/supplement/selenium

81   http://www.webmd.com/vitamins-supplements/ingredientmono-182-manganese.aspx?activeingredientid=182

82   https://www.ncbi.nlm.nih.gov/pubmed/16455317

83   http://orthomolecular.org/library/jom/1984/pdf/1984-v13n02-p105.pdf

84   Philip R. Taylor et al., "Prevention of Esophageal Cancer: The Nutrition Intervention Trials in Linxian, China," *Cancer Research* 54 (7 Suppl)(1994): 2029s–2031s. PMID 8137333.

85   http://billingsgazette.com/news/state-and-regional/wyoming/geysers-fluoride-shortens-elk-life-span-naturally-occurring-element-weakens/article_cd8ae4da-3146-52a2-8f71-0a3ff14dd931.html

86   http://fluoridealert.org/studies/bone01/

87   https://www.cdc.gov/nchs/data/databriefs/db53.htm

88   http://www.annualreviews.org/doi/abs/10.1146/annurev.mi.31.100177.000543

89   Jason Lloyd-Price, Galeb Abu-Ali, and Curtis Huttenhower, "The Healthy Human Microbiome," *Genome Medicine* 8 (2016):51. *PMC*. Web. 9 Dec. 2017.

90   https://www.eurekalert.org/pub_releases/2004-06/ru-bid062504.php

91   American College of Allergy, Asthma, and Immunology, "Allergy Facts," http://acaai.org/news/facts-statistics/allergies; Mayo Clinic, "Mayo Clinic Study Implicates Fungus As Cause Of Chronic Sinusitis," *ScienceDaily* (10 September 1999).

92   Genesis 14:18, Leviticus 10:8–9, Judges 19:19, 1 Samuel 16:20, 1 Samuel 17:18, 2 Samuel 17:29, Job 10:10, Isaiah 7:15

93   Exodus 16:1–36, Numbers 11:1–9

94   Deuteronomy 23:12–13

95   D. Pittet, "Improving Adherence to Hand Hygiene Practice: A Multidisciplinary Approach," *Emerging Infectious Diseases* 7(2)(2001):234–240. doi:10.3201/eid0702.700234.

96   https://en.wikipedia.org/wiki/List_of_countries_by_infant_mortality_rate; https://www.cia.gov/library/publications/the-world-factbook/rankorder/2091rank.html

97   Galatians 5:19–21, Romans 8:8, Ephesians 4:22